The Quilt Maniac's
PLAYBOOK

Fuel for the
Quilt Imagination

quilt ma•ni•ac (kwilt máyneeak) *n.*
A person who loves quilting with
unbridled exuberance and zest.

Nicole C. Chambers

Tiger Lily Press

To Aaron

Your marvelous sense of humor is chocolate for the soul.

Acknowledgments

A heartfelt thank you to —

Chuck Snawder, owner of Harbor Bay Home Furnishings, who made all of his beautiful furniture and home accessories available to me while photographing the quilts for this book. You are a kind and generous man.

Pat Chittenden, whose kind heart is the size of Texas. You worked so tirelessly and enthusiastically testing many of the patterns while still taking the time to send a little TLC my way just when I needed it the most.

Linda Peck, for your willingness to roll up your sleeves and quilt like a trooper. It was such a wonderful help to count on your eagle eye to test quilt patterns.

Jane Wise, for volunteering your fabulous talent for putting on bindings as well as your help in making *Celestial Waltz* (and especially for never being mad at me for making a mess of your shop).

Sarah Martin, my favorite budding artist, for sharing your wonderful talent.

Regina Kuliawat and Loretta Denhart, for your encouragement and support.

And especially to Aaron, for your unfaltering faith and love as well as your willingness to take all things in stride.

Editor: Aaron Chambers
Photography: Colin Park, AFP
Cohen & Park Portrait Studio
Illustrations: Diana Martin
Coast Arts & Graphic Design
Nicole Chambers
Sarah Martin

Published by:

Tiger Lily Press
PO Box 740
Depoe Bay, Oregon 97341
(541) 764-2778
www.quiltmaniac.com

Publisher's Cataloging-in-Publication Data

Chambers, Nicole C.
    The quilt maniac's playbook : fuel for the quilt imagination / Nicole C. Chambers. – 1st ed.
    p. cm.
    Includes bibliographical references and index.
    LCCN: 2001116225
    ISBN: 0-9708375-1-8

    1. Patchwork quilts. 2. Patchwork–Patterns.
3. Color in textile crafts. I. Title.

TT835.C43 2001   746.46
                        QBI01-200277

Printed in the United States of America
10 9 8 7 6 5 4 3 2 1

Contents

It's Not a Quilt ... Until it's Quilted

Few would argue that the way a quilt is quilted will have a huge impact on the final appearance and personality of the quilt. While working on this book, it was my good fortune to have these talented machine quilters working their individual magic on my quilts. If you are a little curious to meet them, let me introduce you ...

Marilyn Badger

Oregon Coast Quilting Brookings, Oregon (541) 412-1002

Marilyn Badger has been involved in quiltmaking for 26 years. Her distinctive talent for quilting in combination with her skillful use of the longarm quilting machine, has made her a much sought after quilter and teacher. Although she has spent many years both quilting and teaching, these days she is primarily concentrating her efforts on teaching her impressive skills to other longarm quilters nationwide as well as in Canada and Australia. As a consultant to American Professional Quilting Systems, she has represented them at shows around the country and has appeared on over 20 PBS quilting shows with Kaye Wood and Fons and Porter.

Her personal interests lean towards contemporary quilts. It seems a natural conclusion, considering how beautifully they lend themselves to her unique freehand quilting designs using special threads such as variegated rayons, polyesters, acrylics, and metallics. Some of these quilts have been featured in publications such as *Traditional Quiltworks, Quilters' Newsletter Magazine, Quilting with Fons & Porter, Sew Many Quilts* and books by Margaret Miller, Karen Combs, Kaye Wood, Joyce Drexler and of course yours truly.

Craig Campbell

Grumpy's Quilts, Amity, Oregon

Ask any quilter in the Pacific Northwest about Grumpy and you'll find that no last name is required; everyone knows whom you are talking about. Known for his impeccable style of machine heirloom quilting, he has managed to do what seemed to be impossible with the longarm machine. His quilting career began when he could not find anyone to quilt his tops with the same designs used in traditional quilting. Frustrated by being limited to pantograph designs that were representative of the available machine quilting at the time, Grumpy decided to buy his own machine and do the quilting himself. He worked, perfecting his quilting technique for 6 months. After thousands of hours of practice, he was able to get the desired result and recreate quilting patterns that you would find in fine traditional quilting.

His love of traditional quilting is apparent in his work. Often you will find samples of his personal quilts displayed at the Sisters Quilt Show. Grumpy believes that no quilt should be relegated to being only a utility quilt, but rather that all quilts deserve special quilting. With proper care, any quilt can be used and loved and still be passed down in great condition.

Merline McLaughlin

The Cotton Yard Eugene, Oregon (541) 689-5128

Quilts have been a part of Merline's life as far back as she can recall; her family brought quilts across the country in covered wagons during their migration in the 1850's. As a child, Merline can remember her paternal grandmother making quilt tops on her treadle sewing machine, which she found fascinating. Merline began her own journey as a quiltmaker for relaxation during a time of high stress, but soon discovered it had become a very central facet in her life.

A talented and skilled quilter, Merline enjoys working with her clients, designing the quilting to carry through the ideas that they have pieced together. Her designs help to define as well as enhance what the quiltmaker has begun with their choice of colors, prints and patterns. The rosebud quilting pattern that you see in *Country Manor* began as an idea drawn in the condensation on the shower curtain one morning. Her inspirations come from everywhere.

Kimberly Olerich

Keepsake Creations Fairview, Oregon (503) 669-0461

Kim works out of her home workshop in Fairview, where she resides with her husband, daughter and son. Custom finish work and freestyle quilting techniques are her forte, but she also enjoys doing pantograph designs. Still a little new to longarm quilting, Kim is showing great promise by the fine workmanship apparent in her quilting technique. To get a really good sense of their quilting needs and expectations, she likes to interview customers in person or by telephone. Kim feels it is important to understand her customers' concepts and tastes so the perfect style of quilting can be applied to their quilts. Communication is key to understanding what her customers are envisioning for their quilts, it is as important as the quilting itself.

Donna Larson

Custom Quilting by Donna Eugene, Oregon (541) 343-7194

Donna creates beautiful custom quilting using her Bernina sewing machine. She approaches quilting as an art form, adding design and dimension to the quilt. Careful to preserve the quilter's vision and concept of the quilt, Donna is a good sounding board of what quilting effects would suit the quilt best. By focusing on the style, personality and color combinations of the quilt, she is able to make creative suggestions of thread choices and quilting designs. Many of her clients choose solid or near solid fabrics for the backs of the quilt just so more of the quilting will show. This is fine with Donna because she thinks the back of the quilt should be as beautiful as the front.

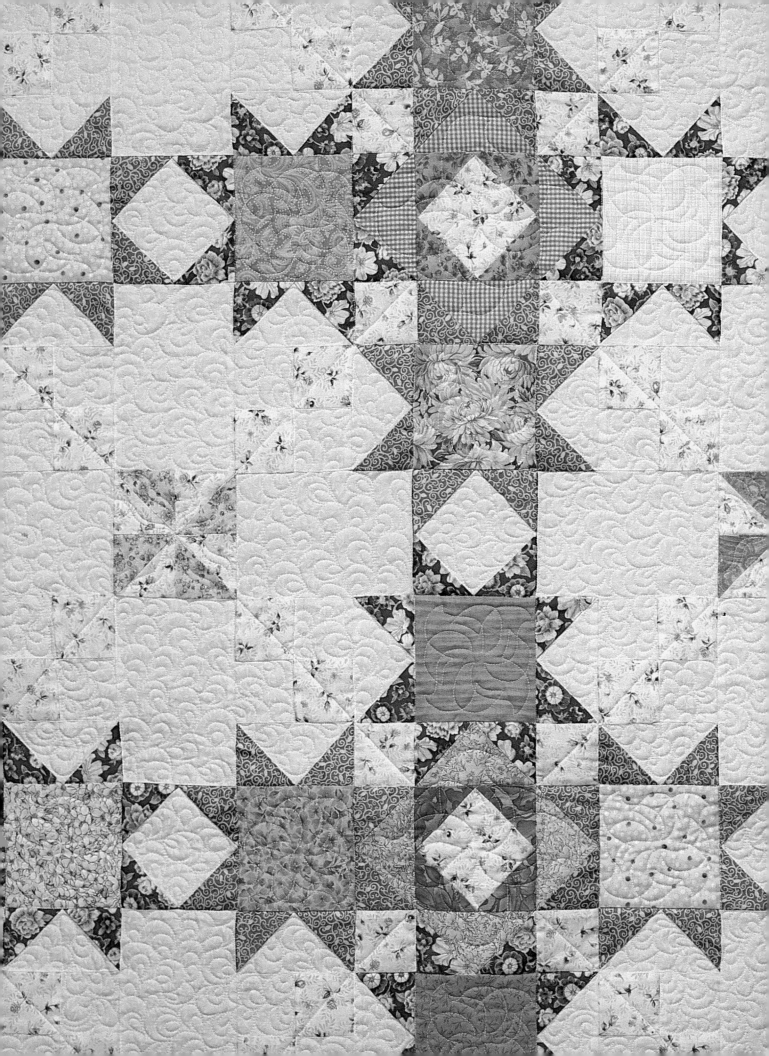

INTRODUCTION

Quilts and fabric. To a quilter it is a never-ending love affair. If the truth be told, more than a few quilters have bought that special book or piece of fabric while mentally adjusting next week's menu to compensate for the dent in the budget. Would they be surprised to find themselves in the impressive company of Michelangelo, Van Gogh and the like? Yes, quilters the same as other artists, need to fuel their imaginations as they passionately practice their art.

Quilting delights our creative spirit. Ideas and inspirations, with pretty bits of cloth, are woven together into a magical assortment of color, texture and love. And we are the magicians at the center of this transformation.

But what if you are not "feeling the magic?" What if deciding on a fabric combination for your next quilt frazzles you until your brain feels like it is actually spinning? Perhaps the quilt you've just finished did not come out quite the way you envisioned and you are feeling disheartened.

Have you ever watched a magician effortlessly make the impossible a reality, right in front of your eyes? How did he do that — you wonder. If you are over the age of 8 (which seems fairly certain by the fact that you are reading this book) you know it wasn't really magic … at least not the … Pooof! you are a frog until you get kissed kind. But rather, by learning what he needed to know and then being shown how to put that knowledge into consistent practice, the magician developed his impressive skills.

Creating quilting magic works very much the same way. Use *The Quilt Maniac's PLAYBOOK* as your trusty guide while you learn to develop your inner artist's eye. Get a clear understanding of how colors interact with each other, and how you can manipulate them to do your bidding. Make the quilts you really love by learning to evaluate prints for not only their graphic elements but also the intangible contributions their personalities make.

Best of all, fuel your imagination with the quilting possibilities this quilt design collection offers. All of the quilts you see in this book are patterns waiting impatiently for you to try them out, for you to put your unique interpretation on them. You'll find that these designs are fully illustrated and have easy to follow step-by-step instructions. They are ready to become the beautiful quilts you envision.

So let's roll up our sleeves and dive into that fabric stash … there are new fabric horizons to explore, and a trunk full of spectacular quilts to make!

COLOR IS ONLY THE BEGINNING

When it comes to color, many quilters have an unrealistic expectation of themselves. If you deposited a dollar in your bank account for every quilter who lamented their lack of color sense, your bank's coffers would be bursting and quite possibly you would be reading this book somewhere on the French Riviera.

For many quilters, having the talent of a good eye for color represents having the knowhow to achieve a glorious color combination almost struggle free. Starting with the spontaneous inspiration of a perfect color scheme, and ending with a trip to their favorite quilt shop — a spectacular quilt unfolds.

The truth is, only in rare circumstances is this scenario possible. The reality is that most talented quilters work quite diligently at combining colors to achieve the envisioned effect.

Let us for a moment imagine that Beethoven and Mozart were quilters rather than musicians. Who can argue with the immensity of their talent? And even if you prefer the music of one over the other, you could not, with any credibility, state that one was better or more talented. From what we know about these very talented artists, it is thought that Mozart was one of the rare individuals who was born with perfect pitch (the musical version of a perfect color sense). He had the ability to literally compose music in his head with such excellence that when he wrote out his compositions, they were nearly flawless. On the occasions that he made any changes, they were for the most part minor and insignificant. As a quilter, it is with certainty and ease that Mr. Mozart would have pulled out a selection of fabrics (how annoying) and the resulting quilt would have been a wonderful and dazzling combination of color.

Beethoven, on the other hand, wrote and then revised and still reworked his compositions even more. Often times, he would work on several significant projects simultaneously, just to give himself a little creative space and keep his objectivity with each one. (Sounds familiar doesn't it?) If Beethoven was a quilter, without a doubt, he would have trashed his favorite quilt shop along with his fabric stash in search of the color combinations that best expressed his inner vision. And even after he found them, he still would have stewed and fussed over them some more. But you can bet the resulting quilt would have been just as wonderful and dazzling.

For most of us, our creative experiences reflect those of Beethoven's rather than those of Mozart's, but to say that because we need to expend a concerted effort to create the color effects we desire means we don't have an *eye for color,* is like saying that Beethoven didn't have a talent for music. It is important that you don't confuse struggling with color combinations and fabric choices and not being good with color as the same thing. In actuality, it is only through this struggle that you gain color experience and become skilled at using color. Each experiment with color and consequently your mistakes with color, is one more notch in your color belt, taking you further on the road to developing and learning to trust the vision of your inner artist's eye.

Developing Your Eye for Color

To develop an eye for color, it is necessary to understand the true nature of color. Color is such a huge part of our existence that we can't even imagine being in a world without it. Yet, we take it fully for granted. We think of it as a constant tangible force of our everyday existence, much like air, the sun, and chocolate. It is so firmly attached to the many objects in our life that we completely overlook its very essence. How many times have you casually said things like, "this is my favorite sweater, I love this shade of red" or "the bright blue cup is mine" expecting those colors to remain rock solid and unchanging? But the true nature of color is that it is intangible. It is like a musical melody or a wonderful aroma, capable of giving us an emotional and physical experience. Our experience with color is not limited to the intellect but rather includes the body, mind, and soul.

The first and most important concept we must grasp is the realization that a color's appearance is never constant. Fire engine red in one color scenario can look more like orange in another, or it can make the blue next to it take on a violet cast while the dusty purple you place across from it can start looking like brown. As colors move in and out of the company of other colors, they never stay the same. Color is always changing or being changed. Its true nature is to be constantly interacting and influencing the colors around it. It is the ultimate chameleon.

At first glance this may sound like terrible news. (A little like trying to walk on a moving floor.) After all, how can one even begin pulling a color combination together if they start jumping around like jumping beans? And the reality is, if you are looking for a short list of concrete rules to follow rather than learning to develop your own sense of color, the experience, indeed, can be a frustrating one.

Learning to develop and trust your artist's eye is a wonderfully freeing adventure. Rather than thinking of color as difficult and

perplexing, think of it as flexible — a magical compound willing and capable to be pushed and pulled into any direction you desire. You only need to understand its character. You will then discover that this chameleon-like nature is in actuality a supple tool, ready to bring your creative ideas to life.

Developing your eye for color means that at times you will have to be patient with yourself and have faith in your abilities, even if at the moment they are not readily apparent. You will need to have the spunk to investigate new waters, to think outside of your comfort zone, acknowledge your color prejudices and be willing to step (or at least tip toe) past them. Mistakes are not failures, but rather your best teachers. You will need the perseverance to work with new color combinations and ideas until they *feel* right. And most importantly, you will need to learn to listen to your inner voice, the one deep down that will tell you when it's just right. In the end, the results are worth the effort a thousand times over. With each accomplishment, your color knowledge will become more firmly rooted, more sophisticated and more experienced. When rules and guidelines aren't giving you the results you want, you'll be able to count on your own eye for color!

So as we start this exciting journey, the first thing you will need to do is dust off your inner voice, the artist's eye. You know, that intuitive part of yourself that you've pushed down and ignored and even maligned for not being very talented while your intellect was busy trying to remember *the right* rules so it could make *the right* choices. It may have gotten a bit rusty and out of shape, but with some encouragement on your part it will become your best assistant and truest advisor. Understanding color requires the work of both the intellect and intuition, but in the end, when all is said and done, it is the artist's eye that always has the last word.

Just in case right at this very moment, that small little voice inside of your head is saying, "what if my artist's eye is out shopping for shoes and has decided not to come back for a while," or worse yet ... "what if I don't have one?" Put your mind at ease. Think back to the last time you found a fabric you really, really loved. Remember as they unrolled it off the bolt, that warm almost giddy feeling in your chest; it nearly made you catch your breath. Proof positive your artist's eye not only exists, it was not off lolly-gagging around somewhere, but was right there giving you a standing ovation!

Understanding the Characteristics of Color

To understand color, you must understand that ultimately its appearance is completely RELATIVE to the colors that surround it as well as highly influenced by the proportion of space each color inhabits. As we investigate the many aspects of color, always keep this very important fact in the back of your mind.

The first question that often arises at the beginning of any quilt project is … "what colors should I use in my quilt?" There are many answers to this question because it rather depends on your reasons for making the quilt. Sometimes it is a simple matter of wanting to show off a favorite fabric. Maybe your much-loved Aunt Millie wants a brown and purple quilt to match her sofa. Other times you just want to make a stunning quilt and simply don't have a clue or even a whisper of inspiration to start with. Take a deep breath … from this moment on resolve to have faith that no matter what colors you finally decide on (or even pick out of a hat), they will have the potential to make a wonderful quilt.

As we become more familiar with the concepts of color, you will find that your faith is well founded. Ultimately, all colors work well together if you understand how to make them bring out the best in each other. As you learn the art and discipline to manipulate color, there is no color scenario that will be beyond your grasp. You will have the ability to make all color combinations look fabulous.

A Rose by Any Other Name …

As we delve into our study of color, you will notice that the terms used are Standard English rather than the *official* color vocabulary (hue, tint, tone etc.). This is not due to anarchism, but rather to make it easier for you to keep your eye on the ball. Some of the concepts examined here are subtle, needing to be visual-ized clearly in your mind's eye. Working with terms that are not everyday familiar requires additional concentration. Since for our discussion it's not crucial to address points pertaining to actual color mixing or scientific points of color, why complicate the issue. This however, does not mean that these facts of color theory are not important. Be encouraged to spend a few hours at the library learning as much about the science of color theory as you can. Knowledge being power applies to understanding color theory as well.

The Balance of Contrast and Unity

Contrast lies at the very heart of our existence. We can't know true happiness if we have never experienced sadness. What is hot if we've never felt cold, the list goes on. Consider what our lives would be like without contrasts. Our existence would be devoid of any interest and variety.

On the other hand, a life of only contrasts would be quite manic. Things would exist only in their extreme states with no middle-ground buffer zone. Things would be loud or silent, brilliant or dull — it's exhausting just to think about it.

So it's not surprising to find that CONTRAST and UNITY are the central components of good design and the heart and soul of making good color choices. It is through this balance of contrasting and unifying color and design elements that we create the quilts of our dreams.

Contrast, for the most part is easily understood. We create contrast by defining or highlighting the differences between the elements involved (in this case, color). Unity, on the other hand, is a little harder to define. Unity is created by building relationships based on similarity, sharing a common denominator among the elements involved. It is important to note that *unifying* elements rather than *matching* them is what achieves good design and color harmony. Many quilt color schemes fall short because this point is overlooked. Unifying elements are free to maintain their individuality while still working together in a cohesive way. Notice that when singers are singing in harmony, they don't all sing the same notes but rather similar notes in different octaves that when heard together form a unified and agreeable sound.

You may be wondering how you will be able to gauge the interaction of these elements as you plan and sew your next quilt. How will you know whether your quilt design contains too many contrasting elements and is visually jarring or has too many similar elements and is bland and boring? How can you know whether you have achieved a good balance of both, creating the beautiful quilt you envision? When the quilt is finally finished and you step back, the moment of truth has arrived. If this is the only time you have evaluated your quilt at a distance — the experience could come as quite a revelation, not to mention a shock. If you develop only one new habit in how you approach choosing colors and fabrics from reading this book, let it be the Rule of 6 Feet. It is the easiest and yet one of the most effective design techniques you can practice. Have you ever heard yourself say, "I'm too close to the problem ... I need a little distance to see more clearly?" Obviously you already know the benefits of this technique.

The Rule of 6 Feet: *Evaluate all aspects of choosing fabrics, as well as where you place them within your quilt design, from a distance of at least 6 feet. Start applying this rule in the quilt shop as you evaluate a fabric's potential and don't stop until all of the design decisions have been made and the quilt is finished.*

You will be amazed at the huge impact this little technique will have on the outcome of your quilts and the education of your artist's eye. What you see at a distance is much more revealing than what you see at 18 inches. Fabrics that are easily differentiated and may even have an attractive soft contrast at close

range will lump themselves together into an indefinable blob of color at a distance. Colors that look eye-catching together at close range may completely lose their spunk from a distance. Get in the habit of using the Rule of 6 Feet in every aspect of quilt design, and use it to make all of your design decisions.

A Quilter's Guide to Using the Color Wheel

If the truth be told, the color wheel is a source of frustration to many quilters. Fabrics are not easily categorized into neat color sections represented on the color wheel and consequently it can be very hard to visualize the many fabric possibilities the pure colors represent. Having said that, know that the color wheel is an important tool to understand and use in managing the many aspects of color.

Think of the color wheel as a cookbook. Some cooks make a lifetime of delicious and memorable meals while their cookbook, for the most part, collects dust on the shelf. Others like to refer to their cookbook occasionally for new ideas and inspirations or perhaps to check on what spices may be the most suitable for a particular dish. While still other cooks really like to give their cookbook a workout, consulting it for almost everything they make. Whatever your style, no kitchen is complete without one; the same is true for the color wheel and the quilter's sewing room. Get one you like and keep it in a handy place. The day will come that it will prove its worth.

As a quilter, the biggest advantage the color wheel offers is that it organizes color combinations in a logical manner. It gives you a good overview of how colors are created (primary, secondary, tertiary), and therefore shows how colors relate to one another. It is a quick reference tool to develop pleasing color combinations, whether you are looking for a complete color scheme or simply locating a color's complement. It can provide the perfect solution to a color problem or even jump-start you with a potential color combination. If you find yourself particularly stuck for an idea, the color wheel can offer a direction you may not have considered. If you are already working on a quilt but find it is coming out lackluster and bland, consulting the color wheel can suggest just the right accent to spunk things up a bit.

Exploring Color Harmony

Just for fun, let's start exploring color harmony by taking a quick spin on the color wheel. As we look at the classic color harmonies of the color wheel, it is important to realize that all colors are represented in their pure form and therefore only supply a part of the color equation. It's with the fine-tuning of value, saturation, temperature and proportion that the true

magic takes place and the individuality of each color combination is realized.

To create color harmony you need to include both unifying and contrasting elements in your color choices. Simply stated, contrast is created when two or more different colors are placed next to each other. How much of a contrast those colors produce depends on their compatibility. Because of the natural lightness of Yellow and deepness of Violet, these colors create the strongest contrast in their pure states; although you can readily change that through the control of saturation and value. On the other hand, to develop unity, you may decide to build color relationships by using colors that share the same temperature or are close neighbors on the color wheel. How much physical space a color family occupies is also an important consideration. It plays a strong role in creating unity as well as providing the perfect opportunity to introduce contrast through the use of other colors.

For the times when there isn't a color idea in your head but your fingers are itching to make a quilt, start by picking one of the classic color harmonies listed below and work from there. Remember that all color harmonies are flexible; they are only a starting point not a rigid roadmap. Absolute obedience is not required or necessary to get a fabulous result. It does not matter if you can't recognize the *official* color scheme you started with, if you love your quilt and it expresses your inner vision, you have triumphed!

As we start this quick tour of the color wheel, think back to the last few quilts you've either made or admired. Chances are you'll recognize their color schemes.

Complementary Color Scheme

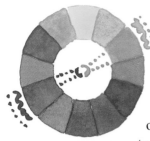

Colors found opposite each other on the color wheel create a complementary color scheme. This color scheme offers the strongest color contrasts, which makes it incredibly fun to work with. Quite certainly you've put this color combination into practice more than once or twice. Most familiar to us during the holidays, it represents the official Christmas colors of red and green. As you look on the color wheel you'll notice that this color scheme offers many other possibilities. When you're feeling a bit adventurous, wander off the beaten path by using colors that are not directly opposite each other as well.

Split-Complementary Color Scheme

When you are feeling even more adventuresome, pick a set of complementary colors and use the two colors on each side of one of the complement rather than the true complement itself. This color scheme consists of at least 3 colors.

Triad Color Scheme

With this color harmony, colors are found equidistant on the color wheel, forming an equally spaced triangle. There is a good chance you will find this color scheme in many of the quilts you have admired. It represents some very popular color combinations such as red, blue and yellow as well as green, purple and orange (peach).

Tetrad Color Scheme

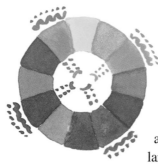

To create this color harmony, use four colors that are found equidistant on the color wheel, forming a square. This color scheme can be interesting and challenging. Remember that not all colors need to be present in large or equal quantities.

Analogous Color Scheme

Colors found adjacent to each other on the color wheel form a natural harmony. We seem to gravitate towards this color scheme with ease and familiarity, probably because we first experimented with it when we were learning to color with crayons. This color scheme always improves if you include at least one color from the opposite color temperature group just to spice things up a bit.

Monochromatic Color Scheme

This color scheme can contain a few or many variations of value and intensity of a single color. It is the Rodney Dangerfield (sometimes getting little respect) of color schemes, although if skillfully handled it can create a beautiful and interesting quilt. If you look at *Days of Wine and Roses* and *Times Remembered* pictured in this book, you will discover that both quilts were created with this color scheme.

As you work with color do not limit yourself to only these classic color scheme ideas. The more comfortable and experienced you become, the more you will realize that essentially all colors can look wonderful together if you control and manage their value, saturation, temperature, as well as their proportions to each other.

Understanding Value

Value is the Big Kahuna, the Big Cheese, the Big Daddy when it comes to color and design. Even if you have quilted for only a short time, quite certainly you have already heard much talk about value. Simply stated, value is the lightness or darkness of a color. Often we think of these graduations as shades. "This shade of blue is lighter than the one you are holding" is a good example of how we generally relate to value.

What makes value such a big player when it comes to designing your quilt is that by its very nature, it sets the stage for all of the other elements you will employ. Value defines what is light, what is dark and what is medium toned in your quilt. It is the traffic cop directing the viewer's eyes as they travel over your finished quilt. How you use value will have a significant effect on how the colors will interact with one another.

More than one colorist has stated that if the value is wrong the color will look wrong. To get a really good understanding of value and how to manage it, let's

visualize a vertical scale numbered from 1 to 10. Be aware that the variations of value far outnumber these limitations, but to make things more manageable let's work with these numbers. The top end of this scale is labeled 10. This is where the color is at its highest value or its lightest point. Technically speaking a 10 would be so light that it would look white with the color presenting itself as only an overtone. The other end of the scale is labeled 1. This number labels the color at its darkest point. Again from a technical standpoint this value would look black with the color showing as an overtone. If you have ever tried to match 2 black fabrics and discovered that one black has a greenish cast while another swings towards the blues, you have seen this firsthand.

To understand how value affects color let's pretend we live in a magical quilt kingdom. In this kingdom colors would come equipped with a value control lever on their side letting you easily experiment with their many settings. You could slide the

lever up and down the scale, trying out all the possible values the particular color has to offer. As you investigated all of the possibilities, you would notice that some colors make dramatic changes as their values change. Yellow is a big surprise for many quilters. At low values it starts turning into an olive green while orange, instead, turns brown. Going to lighter values can have some revelations as well. Often when thinking of light values, our brains immediately visualize pastels, but remember, colors have many value steps before reaching the pastel stage. All of the colors that you have ever seen are a value of one of the pure colors on the color wheel. As you work with different fabrics, challenge yourself to determine (and/or guess) what pure color on the color wheel they belong to.

Unfortunately, to date we don't have magical levers to adjust color values as we design our quilts and so we have to do it manually. You know — by trial and error, considering different fabric combinations until we are satisfied.

Value, as with color, is relative to what surrounds it. A medium blue placed next to a light yellow will be perceived as the dark value, while the same blue next to navy will become the light value; unless of course you also throw in the light yellow. In that combination the blue will become the medium value. Too bad about those levers though; don't you think?

As you work with value, give some thought to the contrasting and harmonious relationships you are creating as well as their proportion to

each other. Where you place light, medium and dark values in your quilt significantly influences how the quilt will look. You can change a quilt design dramatically by simply moving the light, medium and dark values around. Initially the eye sees value before it sees color. Your arrangement of value plays a large part in directing how the eye travels over your design. Skillful use of value will make a stunning quilt no matter what colors you are using. Using value badly can mush your quilt into undefined blobs of color or give it a harsh or disjointed look. Be sure to evaluate all of your value choices with the Rule of 6 Feet. How value is perceived at close range is completely different at a distance.

Sometimes quilters confuse the value of a color with the intensity or saturation of a color. Remember, value speaks to the lightness or darkness of a color whereas a color's saturation speaks to the brightness or dullness of the color. As you gain color experience, this distinction will become much more obvious to you. For now, be mindful that this can be a point of misunderstanding.

Understanding Color Saturation or Intensity

Color saturation, or intensity as it is sometimes called, simply refers to the vividness or dullness of the color. The colors you see represented on the color wheel are thought of as being at their highest point of saturation or intensity. They are in their purest form. Colors that have been softened or dulled such as steel blue or sage green are colors of low intensity and saturation. In essence, color saturation starts at its highest point and is then diluted by softening the color's intensity by graying the color down. Realize that a high intensity color can be as light as a pastel or quite dark. Saturation or intensity refers only to the clearness (absence of gray) or dullness (presence of gray) of a color.

To get a better understanding of how color intensity works, let's again picture another scale, only this time it's a horizontal scale. Again, we will label it from 1 to 10 with the understanding that the possible saturation graduations far outnumber these limitations. On the end of the scale that is labeled 10 is where the color is at its highest point of saturation or intensity. Attaching the magic lever, we again start to push it towards the other end of the scale. As we move away from the end marked 10 we notice that the color starts becoming softer, more muted until we reach 1 where the color is so dulled that it appears to be gray with only an overtone of the color we started with. In this state you could use the color as a neutral, it has so little intensity left. But did you notice something important as you traveled across the saturation scale? Although the color was changing from vivid, to muted, to dull, it did not change its value. It did not get lighter or darker only brighter or duller.

As you begin to work with this concept, be aware that this scale does not only apply to the pure colors, those you see on the color wheel, it also applies to every value each of those colors represent. When you realize the enormous amount of color possibilities this creates it almost takes your breath away ... like when as a kid you first found out where babies came from.

As a rule, most quilters do not often use colors in their most saturated form. Juvenile or novelty prints come close to being a 10 on the saturation scale. Where jewel tones, although still very high in intensity, are often somewhat grayed. Just for fun, collect fabric swatches of pure colors as you come across them. You'll be surprised how grayed some bright looking fabrics really are when you compare them to the pure color swatches. Also, it will train your eye to more easily discern a color's degree of grayness. When you are unsure, place the color in question next to a swatch of the same color that is highly saturated, by the contrast created you will immediately see how much it has been grayed.

Creating contrast by using saturated and grayed shades of the same color can lead to some interesting effects. The saturated color can look almost luminous by contrast of its grayed counterpart. Even when the colors are the same, they may still appear different because of the amount of gray that is present in each. If you examine colors used in prints you will find that many fabric designers use this contrast rather skillfully. Quite often, a single color in a variety of saturations is represented in a print. This gives the print variety and interest without creating visual complexity by using many different colors. When used well, this contrast can make the saturated color come forward while the less saturated colors create interesting background support. Use care in not allowing the proportion of the more intense colors to be too large. Because of their saturation, your eye will be drawn immediately to the areas they inhabit.

Used badly, a highly saturated color combined with another of lower saturation can make the less intense color look downright frumpy while the highly saturated one starts looking garish. In these instances the colors are hostile to each other rather than bringing out each other's best. You can solve this problem by narrowing the saturation gap.

have made significant studies of these effects. The packaging of your favorite products are not colored at the whim of the designer, but rather based on scientific data. In a simple test, when test subjects were placed in rooms painted with cool colors, they reported the perceived room temperature to be lower than the actual temperature. While in rooms painted with warm colors, the same test subjects perceived the temperature to be higher even though the actual temperatures of all rooms were identical. Something to think about the next time you need to paint that cold hallway. It was also found that while the test subjects were soothed and calmed by the cool colors, warm colors energized, excited and even agitated them.

If you have ever needed to match 2 or 3 blues together, quite likely you came away from the experience thinking that there must be a gazillion medium blues out there — and none of them compatible with each other. Even though you looked only at blues with a similar value, the reason they were not matching was likely due to a mismatch in color saturation. But it is also quite possible another attribute of color, that of color temperature, may have been the culprit.

Understanding Temperature

Scientists and psychologists have long been fascinated with the physical and emotional responses human beings have to color. It is no secret that in order to gain the best marketing advantage, many industries

As you know, color temperature is a visual perception rather than color actually producing heat or cold. Each color on the color wheel has been assigned to belong to either a warm or cool color group. As you look at the color wheel, you will notice that half of the colors: the reds, oranges and yellows belong to the warm group while the: blues, greens and violets belong to the cool group.

Understanding how color temperature affects your quilt design can be a very useful tool. Since cool colors recede and warm colors come forward, you can create interesting visual perceptions. As you work to create color schemes, you will find that most color combinations only improve when they include both warm and cool colors. It is good design strategy to give your quilt a dominant color temperature and then use colors from the opposite color temperature in smaller amounts rather than using color temperatures in equal proportions. Varying the ratio of warm and cool temperatures adds interest where equal divisions (as with other design elements) make the quilt look static.

Fabric designers have found that contrasts created by opposing temperatures can be a useful design tool. Take time to notice this type of contrast the next time you are looking at fabric. Wonderful soft contrasts can be created without giving up shape definition as well as producing contrasts that make strong energetic color statements.

Understanding color temperature would be a slam-dunk if that was all there was to it. All you would have to do is figure out which colors are warm, which are cool and you're home free, right? Well ... some horse holding is in order with that thought. Aside from colors being assigned a warm or cool family group, each shade of color, no matter what family it is designated to, will have a warm or cool undertone. To understand this better, visualize a magic toggle switch (much like a light switch) marked *warm* and *cool* attached to the side of each color. If you flip the switch to warm, the color will start to have a warm (yellowish) undertone. If you flip

switch to cool, the color will start taking on a cool (bluish or violet) undertone. But remember, how warm or cool a color appears is highly influenced by the quantity and strength of the color temperature that surrounds it.

As you work with fabric colors, spend a few seconds considering the warm and cool undertones of the colors you are using. These undertones can be very subtle or they can be quite obvious depending on the color. In many instances adjusting the cool or warm undertone of a color is all that is needed to make warring colors start looking harmonious. Think back on a time you may have added a warm blue to your quilt and suddenly the other blues started to look downright unattractive. Or maybe it was the other way around and the blue you added began to look lost and forlorn. Use color temperature to create mood, to create contrast or to create a harmonious and lively color scheme for your next quilt.

Using Neutrals in Color & Design

Technically speaking, white, black and gray are considered true neutral colors. In quilting, it is safe to expand neutrals to also include off-white and all colors of very low saturation.

Using these neutrals wisely can intensify or defuse color combinations. For instance, a color of medium value and saturation when placed against a black background will start to look much livelier. Whereas, the same color against a white background can make the color look lackluster. Very soft colors placed on a black background will wash out, while a white background will create just the right amount of contrast to show the colors at their best. Highly saturated colors placed with gray will noticeably mellow them, creating an interesting soft yet lively effect.

But along side of neutral colors, we must also consider how to use neutral design space, intertwining these elements to create an overall harmony in our quilts. We need neutral space and color in our quilts to give our eyes a place to rest. In quilts that do not provide this rest oasis, our eyes will keep jumping from place to place, never stopping on any one thing.

This creates too much visual information for our brains to process all at once. Rather than trying to figure things out, our brain stops deciphering any of the information. Consequently we lose interest and look for something else to capture our attention. Think back on the last time you looked at something that was so busy you couldn't be bothered trying to figure out what it really was. That was your brain stepping out to get a cup of coffee.

By providing a place for the eye to rest, you create a contrast between areas of high interest, which are your strong colors and/or high design sections, with areas of low interest, which are the neutral colors and/or low design sections. Our brain

now happily processes the information with gusto and we experience joy and interest as we look at the quilt. Thoughtful use of neutral colors and design areas can make the difference between a glorious quilt design and one that is merely mediocre.

We as quilters however, would be doing ourselves a disservice if we only thought in terms of using neutral colors in neutral design areas such as the background of the quilt. Many quilt designs and color schemes benefit from a much more interactive approach. Take for instance *Intrigue on the Orient Express*. The background, which is often relegated to the neutral zone in terms of color, is in this case a soft but somewhat saturated peach. Since this fabric is used in such a large proportion the color seems even more intensified. The absence of an obvious pattern however makes it a good candidate for the neutral design area, providing a rather lively place for the eye to rest. The peach fabric however would have easily become overwhelming if other fabrics in the quilt didn't provide some degree of neutrality to diffuse and balance the color scheme. In this case, the theme fabric as well as a supporting fabric is printed on a black background. If the background of either of these fabrics had been a color rather than the strong neutral black, using the peach would have put this color scheme over the top with too much color and the effectiveness of the quilt design would have been lost.

In many quilts, neutrals don't get the respect they deserve, getting tossed in as more of an afterthought than a design aspect. Take the time to really consider how and where using neutral design spaces and neutral colors will benefit your quilt. Study how other quilters have used these neutral elements in quilts you admire and think about how you could adapt those concepts in your quilts. Make it a point to place neutral colors and neutral design spaces in your quilts with purpose rather than by default.

A Hands-On Approach to Color

Whew! We have covered a lot of information since we started this chapter. Now that you have familiarized yourself with many aspects of color and the important part they play, it is time for you to really learn how to become skilled with color. Ultimately, using color well can only be learned through experience. It is much like learning to drive a car. You can read technical manuals until the cows come home, you can know all the rules of the road by heart, but until you get into the car, turn the ignition key, and let the rubber

meet the road, you will never learn to drive. Only by practicing driving will you ever become a good driver. The same is true with color. Knowledge is the very necessary starting point, but only by actually working with it, gaining experience with it, will you become really good at handling color. So roll up your sleeves and don't worry … you will learn a technique that makes it fun, fun, fun!

A Visit from Your Very Own QFG

What if, as you started planning your next quilt, your very own Quilt Fairy Godmother made an appearance? More amazingly, what if she offered you a deal — one you couldn't refuse. If you gave up a couple inches of your fabrics along with the promise of using your noodle implementing all this color stuff you have learned, YOU would end up with the quilt of your dreams — would you jump at the chance?

In case you are worrying about those couple inches of fabric you are asked to give up, consider what would happen if all the quilters in the world came together and piled their stashes in one spot. The pile would be so huge that the sheer weight of it would probably pull the earth out of its orbit. Fabric is your medium to create beautiful and wonderful quilts and even your most favorite fabrics will be much happier showing themselves off in a beautiful quilt rather than waiting patiently in a box or on a shelf for the next time you will pet them. There will always be more wonderful and gorgeous fabric for you to buy and love! Giving up a few inches is a small price to pay for developing your artist's eye and making quilts you really love.

Using a Personal Design Board

No matter how long you've been quilting, no matter how good you are with color and design, in the end you are not going to really know how well a new color combination is going to work until you actually see it in the fabrics you want to use. It's hard to be daring if the price of being an adventurer is a quilt you don't like. But it is equally heartbreaking to discover that after investing your time, effort and money your quilt does not quite hit the mark. Without active experimenting and trying new concepts, how will you ever be able to develop your eye for color? How will you grow as a quilter? On the other hand, how do you gain this experience without the risk of making quilts you dislike?

What makes using the personal design board so valuable is that it gives you the freedom to try

ANYTHING without consuming your valuable time with a lot of unnecessary fussing around. Neither are you committed to sewing test blocks or making an entire quilt just to see if your idea will work. You will find the personal design board is your most influential teacher as you develop your own personal style. It is the classroom of your artist's eye, and best of all it is as fast as it is easy.

A personal design board is simply your personal 16-inch portable design wall. Its compact size is practical for testing blocks, keeping everything conveniently next to your cutting mat as you work out your color ideas. The fabric will stick to the board so you simply need to place the pieces where you want; no sewing will be needed to test your ideas. It is easily propped up just about anywhere so you can evaluate your progress with the Rule of 6 Feet no matter how limited your sewing space may be. Plus you can carry it around with you just in case you need to scrounge some fabric from your friends.

To start, select the fabrics you think will work well for the quilt you are planning, but keep lots of other choices around to experiment with as well. From your selection, cut out the pieces you will need to make one block. Instead of cutting pieces the size specified in the cutting instructions, do not include any seam allowance. As you try out your various fabric candidates in your quilt block, you are going to work in finished sizes. So if the instructions say you need a 2½" square (unfinished), you will cut a 2" square. If the instructions want you to use a triangle that was created from cutting a square in half once, subtract ⁷⁄₈" from the cutting instructions, while triangles that are created by cutting squares in half twice, subtract 1¼" — you get the idea. Don't worry if the pieces are not perfect, this is your test lab for working out your color schemes and fabric ideas.

Experiment with the fabrics you have chosen; place them in areas that seem best to you. Prop your personal design board up and evaluate your combination with the Rule of 6 Feet. Does one fabric look washed out, or is it too brash? Replace it with stronger or softer colors. Do you need to shift the values around a little? Experiment and see how they will look in different places. Do you wonder what effect another fabric or new color would have? Try many colors and many fabrics. Would stripes look good in a section? Find stripes and in a minute you will know. Try EVERYTHING! The more you work manipulating fabrics and color on the personal design board, the more experience you are gaining. Don't be afraid to put some odd things together or fabrics you think might look ugly together. Seeing what doesn't work is as important as finding things that do. Try everything that seems right to you until your inner voice tells you that what you have put together hits the bull's eye dead on.

You are ready to start your quilt! As an extra bonus you will find that all of your experimenting has also made you quite familiar with the construction concepts of the block. What fun you will have at the sewing machine. This time you won't be disappointed.

When you are finished, you will love your quilt because all of the experimenting has been done live and in living color. The fabrics you have evaluated and decided on are exactly the same in size and color as what was used in your quilt. That little voice will not be wondering what if ... because you will already know. The personal design board is not quite as good as having magic levers, but it is the next best thing! You will be amazed at the difference it will make in your quilts.

Making a Personal Design Board is Easy

You will find that making a personal design board is very, very easy. Simply follow the instructions below and in no time at all you will have this wonderful tool at your disposal.

On a 16″ square of ¼″ foam core board, glue an 18″ square of thin cotton batting onto one side of it. Let it dry thoroughly and trim the batting flush with the foam core square.

To use color to its best advantage requires knowledge, judgment and intuition. It is a discipline and an art. With this little design board and your continued efforts to improve your quilting skills, you will learn to balance color, value, intensity and temperature to get the results you want. As we continue our journey and explore the world of prints, this tool will prove to be even more valuable. What a fun way to develop your artist's eye and learn to trust your intuitions!

TEXTURES, PRINTS & PERSONALITY
The Other Half of the Fabric Equation

The human eye can perceive 10 million variations of color. Sometimes it seems that fabric manufacturers are printing 9 million of them, doesn't it? Never before have quilters enjoyed such an abundance of fabric choices. The fabrics wave and twinkle, vying for our attention. And how can we resist? We love them all.

If time travel was possible, just imagine how quilters from 100 years ago would react as they stepped into our quilt shops which are literally stuffed with prints of every color and pattern. You can be sure that smelling salts would have to be standard equipment in every quilt shop worldwide. We truly live in an age of abundance. It's hard to believe that at one time the formulation of certain dyes and pigments were so rigorously guarded that revealing their secret was punishable by death. With the skyrocketing growth of color technology today, we live in an age of unprecedented fabric prosperity. But along with the sheer joy of having such an abundance of variety and choice comes the anxiety of choosing well. With so many fabrics abound, how is it possible to find just the right ones for our quilts?

Let us examine the characteristics that make up prints and learn how we can use them to create the looks we love.

What Color is the Print?

It's the first question that comes to mind as we first examine a piece of printed fabric. With some fabrics such as tone-on-tone prints and textures, a fairly casual look will reveal its overall color. But with many prints it becomes a more complex issue. Depending on many factors within the print itself, the color you would classify it as when looking at it close up will not necessarily be the same color it appears to be at a distance. That is why it is so important to evaluate all fabrics with the Rule of 6 Feet.

By viewing fabrics at a distance, the overall color effect of a print will become much more readily apparent. What may look like red with blue squiggles up close can look purple at a distance if the squiggles are small and closely placed. If the squiggles are further apart and larger, your eye will easily identify the squiggle pattern as separate from the background but the red will look much deeper than what it appears to be at close range. Remember everything you have learned about the interaction of color. These factors do not only apply to the colors you are putting together for your quilt. They are also forces at work within the print you are evaluating. The colors are

Then again, not all prints create a definable color effect. In instances where the motif is large enough to be easily identified at a distance, the print will show its many colors without seeming to blend them together. You probably have a fair number of fabrics in this category. What makes them perplexing to work with is also what makes them so interesting and appealing. Sometimes the only choice you have is to work with them in terms of value or what is also referred to as visual weight. Remember, perceived value (or visual weight) is dependent on what you place around the fabric in question so be sure to evaluate the print in that context.

influencing one another and thus producing a unique color effect. It is this effect, rather than the individual ingredients of the pattern, that you are interested in. If you ever look at an impressionist's painting really close up, you will notice that it is a multitude of dots in different colors. From a distance, your eyes visually mix these dots and you see the beautiful picture the artist created. The actual colors of the dots become meaningless, only the overall effect they create is significant.

As you evaluate fabric at a distance, look for any distracting aspects the print may have. What are cute little white bunnies up close can look like white blobs at a distance. White in particular attracts the eye so pay special attention if and where it exists in a print. Also, look for any particularly strong color elements in a pattern. Close up they may be charming little purple flowers but at a distance your quilt could look like it has chicken pox.

When working with prints, use everything you have learned about color. The same principles still apply only now the extra dimensions of visual texture, print design and personality have been added to the mix.

Exploring the Characteristics of Prints

Aside from color, it is the motif, or the central design, that first attracts us to a fabric. The motif is the heart of the fabric. Aside from color, it's the strongest influence in setting the tone of the fabric's personality and style. From the multitude of fabric choices that exist, you could hardly name a subject or geometric shape that is not addressed as a fabric motif in some fashion.

Since the motif is so central to the identity of a print, it offers an excellent place to start our exploration. As you look at the design of a fabric, evaluate whether the motif is generally round or angular. With some fabrics the answer is obvious but many fabrics are a combination of both. Some prints are fairly geometric with some round or curving influences while others are primarily round with some angles. In either case, get a feel for the overall roundness or angularness of the motif. Don't overlook texture prints in your evaluations. Some textures have such a nondescript pattern that they easily combine with almost all print styles, while others have a definite curved or angular feel to them. Even though tone-on-tone prints are subtle, in many instances their motifs are surprisingly noticeable at a distance.

One of the secrets of combining interesting and successful prints together is to create contrast and unity with the graphic shapes of prints in addition to those you create through the use of color. If defining the graphic elements of prints is confusing for you, make black and white copies of the fabrics you are working with on the copier. The absence of color will easily separate the graphic shapes from the color attributes of the fabrics.

As we discussed earlier, contrast is created by defining and highlighting the differences of the elements involved, which in this case are the round or geometric motifs featured in the print. A classic example of creating graphic contrast is combining florals, which are primarily rounded shapes, with stripes or plaids, which are strong geometric shapes.

To create, unity you need to build relationships based on commonality among the elements involved. Although many quilters intuitively build unity by echoing graphic elements in the prints they choose, a common mistake new quilters make is not including enough variety in motif size or what is also called *print scale*. This creates too much visual sameness, which in many instances fails to make an interesting combination of patterns. Be sure to include a mixed selection of print sizes when you choose your fabrics.

Large-scale prints can offer some interesting benefits as well as some disadvantages. The large-scale print, when cut up, offers many color and graphic possibilities. One fabric can even take on the look of half a dozen. On the other hand, a large print can also cut up to make the pieces look disjointed. Don't let that discourage you from trying them. By using your personal design board, you can experiment with all print scales and educate your artist's eye to create the look you love.

Another question that needs to be answered is how the motif spaced. Some fabric patterns melt completely together. You can't really tell where the motif starts or where it ends. These fabrics are usually very easy to use and work well in many situations. Other fabrics are printed at regular (geometrically spaced) or random intervals with varying degrees of background showing. These fabrics are a little more mysterious as to how they will look when cut up. You will need to consider the background color and value of these fabrics with care. When cut up, they may show quite a bit of the background and very little motif. If the background blends easily with your other fabrics, you will lose the definition of your block design. This could have significant consequences if the print is placed in key design areas, such as star points for instance. Even at small distances, the star points could visually melt into the other fabrics around it and the design of the quilt would be lost. In addition, the bits of motif that do show may make the eye travel in odd contortions and give the quilt design an incoherent look.

How a motif is spaced can also offer some interesting design options to consider. Round shapes with very geometric spacing such as classic polka dots, can look decidedly geometric even though the motif is round. If you are a quilter that doesn't like geometric prints to be cut *off kilter*, you will want to pay particular attention to this type of spacing. Another aspect to observe is that although some motifs that are regularly spaced and cut up beautifully, they can create an unattractive overall pattern when a large amount of the fabric is showing (such as in borders). This will be easy to spot at a distance so remember to evaluate fabric with the Rule of 6 Feet.

Some fabrics are printed with a one or two-way design. Many quilters shy away from using these because they think they'll be difficult to use. This is unfortunate. These fabrics can create fabulous effects. Often they add an exciting sense of movement in many areas of a quilt. Be sure to include these when you experiment with combining patterns.

Visual weight is to prints what value is to color. Since prints are a combination of many single ingredients, you will need to evaluate the visual density or visual weight of the fabric print in its entirety. Visual weight is highly influenced by both the overall density of the print as well as the colors involved. The darker and/or denser a print appears, the more visual weight it will have. Use visual weight in the same way you use value. The placement of these fabrics is important to the design of your quilt. If you use prints that do not have enough visual weight, the overall quilt design can look disjointed. The next time you have difficulty discerning the design of certain quilt blocks, check to see if they are suffering from not enough visual weight in these key places.

One thing that prints really bring out in most quilters is an overwhelming desire to *match* other fabrics to the print. If the print has tiny little rust flowers on it, many quilters cannot resist the temptation to scour the quilt shop for a perfectly matching rust. Even if the exact shade of rust is found, there are much better alternatives. Remember all you have learned about the chameleon-like qualities of color? A burgundy could prove to be a much better choice, giving your quilt the zing it needs while the perfectly matched rust could easily look perfectly boring. You already know that once you put burgundy next to the flowers they will magically start to look burgundy themselves.

More quilters do an injustice to their quilt designs by matching too many things than anything else they do. The next time you find yourself *matching* (and we all do it at one time or another) remember this scenario. Your favorite Aunt Sally is coming to visit and you want to make her favorite dish, honey chicken. She has told you that there is no one in the family that makes honey chicken as tasty as you do, so you know this is going to be a great menu idea. You want the whole meal to be a big hit so you start planning the rest of the menu with enthusiasm.

If you apply the matching mindset as you plan the rest of the meal, you may end up with a menu that would start with, let's say … chicken noodle soup. For the salad you could have chicken salad with honey mustard dressing and to the main entrée you could add candied sweet potatoes and glazed carrots. Oh yes, you don't want to forget the honeydew slices to garnish the honey chicken and perhaps even add some honey biscuits. You can readily see that this menu is becoming not only boring but also overwhelmingly monotonous rather than the wonderful meal you were envisioning. Matching takes on a whole different look when you think about it in terms of food, doesn't it? Interestingly, what creates good food harmonies (balance of contrasting and unifying tastes and textures) are the same principles for creating great harmonies with fabric. Chances are, you could easily come up with menu ideas to complement the honey chicken, offering a mix of tastes and textures to harmonize rather than oppress with similarity. Use that same mindset when you are putting fabrics together for your quilt, and draw on all that matching energy to create harmony by using differences to create contrast and relationships based on common elements to build unity.

Defining the Personality of Prints

Defining a print's personality can be tricky business and in the end, the final answer rests on your personal interpretation of how the fabric speaks to you. But to start our exploration of defining this elusive character, let's look at some important elements that have a strong influence on forming the personality of a print.

These days we have a choice of fabrics printed in an almost endless variety of themes or subject matters. Quite literally we have everything from flying pigs and Elvis to the most impressive collection of flora and fauna ever printed on textiles. Although the subject matter of a print is not *the* defining factor, it is an important ingredient in the personality mix. Judging from their subject, it becomes obvious that some prints have a sense of humor and fun while others are steeped in history and tradition. Some favor the great outdoors and still others want nothing more than hearth and home. And let us not forget the men of mystery, the indefinable subjects that pride themselves in remaining an enigma thus lending themselves completely to our interpretations of them.

What influences the personality of a print more than anything else is the style in which the textile designer chose to portray the subject matter. As we begin to notice the many styles fabrics are rendered in, the personality of the print starts coming into the forefront. A floral can be made to look very traditional or be so highly stylized that it borders on the avant garde. Some florals look realistic enough to be mistaken for a photograph rather than an artist's representation, while still others only barely reflect the image of a flower at all.

Further into this mix is color. Some color combinations or intensities can reflect an important side of the personality and must be considered. Print designs rendered in low intensity colors can look vintage or soft, while others because their color intensity is so high, can start looking fun even though the motifs are very similar. Brilliant colors make most prints look happy, fun, and in many cases, add a contemporary feel to them.

As you explore the many nuances of fabric personality, you may be wondering to yourself how you will ever manage to work with so many fabric personalities. It may amuse you to know that many of the same skills you use in managing the varied personalities of your friends, relatives, and acquaintances will serve you well when you apply them to the fabric personalities you are considering for your next quilt. But when a friend tells you what a great personality her fabric has, don't be tempted to think it is ugly.

To get the idea, let's start asking a few questions to see what we can learn about fabric personalities and how they may reflect the personalities of people in your life.

Is the Print Open Minded or … High Maintenance?

Is the print flexible or completely limited to how and where it can be used or perhaps something in the middle? You may have a friend who wouldn't know a hockey puck from an Oreo cookie or a dinosaur bone from a chicken bone. If you invited her to accompany you to a sports event or the museum, she would quite

likely not need very much coaxing. She would go with the intention of having fun as well as being good company for everyone around. This friend is open to new experiences and easily adapts to many different and unfamiliar situations, which explains the many invitations that come her way.

On the other side of the scale, we all know someone (most likely a relative) who has to have things their way or they will never stop telling you how unhappy they are. This personality will only participate happily in a very limited number of situations and only under certain conditions. It's best not to coax her into something that is outside of her comfort zone because in the end you will find yourself standing on your head just to make her happy. Usually it's not worth all the extra effort. Best to let them stay in situations they are the happiest in.

Others can be coaxed into a situation if some of their friends are going to be there as well. With friends around them, they will make the best of most situations and often end up becoming good company even if it started out as not really their thing.

Fabric personalities work very much the same way. There are some that are very flexible. They will look wonderful in a wide variety of combinations and quilts. Others do not travel easily outside of their style group at all. It is best to use them within the limited groups they are happiest in. And the ones in the middle can often be coaxed into looking well if you partner them up with other fabrics of their genre.

Is the Print a Talker or a Listener?

Maybe your Uncle Bob is a real talker. And although he tells the most riveting and exciting stories, the truth is he just talks, and talks and talks. Usually he has so much to say, you can't get a word in edgewise. Uncle Bob needs to be the center of attention and trying to make him hush up even for a little bit just isn't going to work. At your next get-together, you better not seat him next you your Aunt Bessie who is somewhat of a gabber herself. She doesn't talk as much as Uncle Bob but they'll still spend the whole evening in conflict; each trying to talk while neither one showing the slightest inclination of listening to what anyone else has to say. On the other hand, your friend Henrietta can never be accused for being at a loss for words but is also quite happy to listen when an interesting subject is brought up. She doesn't have to hog the limelight to be happy. If you seat her next to your Uncle Bob, they will most likely get along very well. Henrietta's strong conversational skills may even make Uncle Bob feel so appreciated that he will be at his best, most entertaining self ... even if he does do all the talking.

Also quite likely, you have some very lovable friends who don't have strong conversational skills, preferring situations that are a little lower key. In most situations they will be happy to contribute to the group, but if the conversation gets too intense they just sit there being bored and rolling their eyes rather than actually participating in the conversation. If you place them next to people who are a little less intense, willing to talk less and listen more, they will happily participate by adding to the conversation. As you look at prints, note which ones are the talkers, which ones are the listeners and which ones know how to talk as well as listen. Some fabrics will need to be the center of attention while others only want a part of the limelight. Some fabrics don't have enough going on within them and become overwhelmed by strong prints. Evaluate how much of a talker or listener they are and arrange them accordingly.

When you are at a loss of how to handle fabric personalities, use your people skills to help you make the decisions. Ask yourself how the personality attributes of the fabric could translate onto a person. Does the fabric give off an air of being prim and proper or is it more of a party girl? Does it need to be a comedian or is it more of a serious intellectual? Relating fabric to people is not only fun, it also opens the door to actively thinking about the personalities of the fabrics you are working with. This way of thinking will offer help when you need to decide whether or not a fabric fits within the personality mix of your quilt and where within that quilt they will be most happily situated. Fabric combinations thrive in a mix much the same as people. Let that be your guide. You know that people enjoy diverse and interesting company where they feel a sense of comfort because they also share some common interests with others in that group. What a fun way to create contrast and unity with prints.

Putting Fabrics Together

Many quilters feel it is a failing on their part if they cannot visualize in their mind's eye how fabrics will look when put together into a quilt. In a small corner of their heart, they hang onto the feeling that if they were really good at it, they would be able to imagine the effect the fabrics will create.

As you have learned, building successful fabric combinations is more involved than simply putting fabrics you like together. Rather, it is a blending of their many characteristics of color, pattern and personality that creates the look you are working to achieve. Add to that the extra mystique of how the fabrics will look *cut up* and you have a real brainteaser. This is what makes quilting exciting, and sometimes frustrating, and incredibly interesting as well as a little anxiety producing and completely fascinating — but you know all that.

Believe it or not, you are much more skilled at making fabric choices than what you give yourself credit for, but you must give yourself something to work with. Trying to imagine the many variables and possibilities a group of fabrics present is asking a lot of your mind's eye. This is why seeing the actual fabrics working together as you take them for a test run on your personal design board is so important. It gives your artist's eye something to work with. Evaluating whole pieces of fabric on a design wall is

a good start but it will not show you the effect they will produce when cut up. Fabrics can take on completely different looks and personalities depending on the shape they are cut into, the size of that shape and where within the quilt design they are placed. They add subtle and unexpected influences.

If there are only 2 new habits you acquire from reading this book, let the second one be using your personal design board to experiment with color and pattern ideas as you test run fabric possibilities. What it will teach you about combining fabrics, you will not learn anywhere else.

EXPLORING
THE POSSIBILITIES

Too many people think that you just sit down and make a quilt ... a quilt evolves. It can start out as a swatch of fabric or a picture or even just a vague memory of a particular time in your life. No matter where the inspiration originates, as the quilt becomes a reality, it takes on a life and personality of its own. Quiltmaking is both a creative avenue of self-expression and a way of sharing love. Is it really any surprise that quiltmakers will go to almost any length to rescue any and all quilts relegated to a damp basement or the garbage bin? No matter what their condition, the quilt can somehow be saved or recycled, continuing its existence in some fashion, still being appreciated in some manner.

The Evolution of a Quilt

There are many paths quilts take as they are created. It is almost a certainty that you will zig and zag, this way and that, until it all fits into place and the quilt comes together. Just for fun, follow me as we retrace the path that ended up becoming *In Search of Hemingway*.

In Search of Hemingway started out with the green swatch of fabric you see below. This fabric insisted on coming home with me from the local quilt shop and even though it was obvious that my enthusiasm for it was somewhat lost on others; I loved this fabric. It whispered to me in a way that sparked a long forgotten memory of high school wardrobes and my love for leopard prints — which at that time had manifested itself into *the leopard dress*. Some people may find it hard to imagine, but in those days Tina Turner and I could have easily shared the same closet.

Just as visions of animal prints were dancing around in my head, almost by magic these perfect animal prints crossed my path and immediately became part of this quilt.

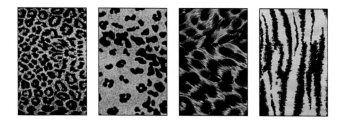

The animal prints were perfect for the quilt, but as you may have noticed, they also had too much visual weight and color intensity to be paired with the original green jungle fabric. In their company, it looked overwhelmed, washed out, and bored. The jungle fabric was replaced with the stronger conversationalists you see below.

The quilt was really starting to take shape but it was still missing a few fabrics. In my continued search, the ethnic print below stirred some ideas. It didn't have the right personality to be included into the mix, but it sparked the idea of using a combination of the gold and green fabrics shown below.

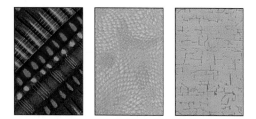

Notice that the finished quilt doesn't have any of the apple green. When evaluating these fabrics with the Rule of 6 Feet, the green defused the color scheme of the quilt with too much similarity. The gold, on the other hand, made the other fabrics come alive. The obvious answer was to add a variety of golds.

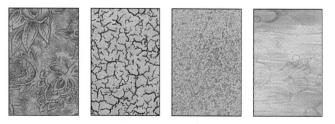

The red and black fabrics just about came to the door on their own volition and asked to join the party. They were an obvious choice when you consider the black added contrast and worked beautifully as a neutralizing influence since this quilt was starting to make a strong color statement. The red fabric offered an interesting contrast, the perfect accent to the predominantly green color scheme.

The floral fabric in the animal blocks was added as a point of interest. It was chosen for its contributions in terms of color, graphic design and personality. Since this flower print contained a fair amount of purple, the squares were strategically cut so that it would show only at a minimum.

This is how the creative path zigged and zagged and *In Search of Hemingway* came to be.

Learning to See the Possibilities

But what if ... as you looked at a picture of this quilt you had said to yourself "I don't really like using animal prints" and then turned the page. You would have missed the opportunity of giving this quilt your personal interpretation and creating something completely different and wonderful.

My friend, Linda Peck is an artist when it comes to making scrappy country quilts. She is the Queen of Country, so it should come as no surprise that animal prints are not exactly her thing. Looking past that interpretation of the quilt design, she saw strikingly different possibilities. Notice how her choices of fabric and color have given *Country Manor* a completely different personality even though it is made from exactly the same pattern. Every quilt, no matter where the inspiration comes from, takes on a unique personality. It is up to you to look past the obvious of what is — to see the possibilities of what can be.

Learning to see the possibilities rather than just the obvious is a very important part of growing as a quilter. If you look at quilts by singularly observing only what you like and dislike, you will come away

from the experience with exactly what you already know — what you like and don't like. Instead, let these opportunities become occasions to enrich your artist's eye, to learn more about the use of color, texture and fabric and ultimately to become a better quilter!

Teach yourself to observe the relationships of color, value, intensity, temperature as well as their proportions. Actively think about the personalities of the fabrics and how they are grouped. Learn to understand the underpinnings of the quilt rather than simply giving it a superficial overview. Ask yourself questions. How and what is being used to create unifying relationships? What is creating contrast? How are the neutral colors and neutral design spaces being used? Study how the prints, textures, and colors work together as a whole. What is their common denominator and how are they strikingly different? Looking at the quilt, evaluate all these elements rather than concentrating only on the colors. You may not like the colors of that particular quilt but if you understand how the elements interrelate, you will have the expertise to make a beautiful quilt no matter what color scheme you decide on.

Start stretching your creativity this way every chance you get. After you've looked at the quilts in this book, turn to the black and white graphic of each quilt design. You will find them included with the step-by-step instructions, and start to dream a little. What colors would you use — what fabrics? If you close yourself off from a quilt design because you do not like green or purple or florals or animal prints, look at the creative quilting opportunities you will be missing.

In instances where you love the colors and fabrics that were used in the quilt and want to make one just like it, pay special attention to not only the colors, but their nuances as well. If the fabric is pink, is it a peachy pink with warm undertones or

carnation pink with cool undertones. Is the pink a clear pink or has it been grayed? What is the pink next to, is it a cool or warm burgundy? What style of print is the burgundy and how does it compare to the pink? If the pink is a floral, ask yourself what is the personality of the floral? Is it a contemporary sophisticated type or does it exude old world southern charm? What floral could you use that would keep the integrity of the overall quilt personality? How do the fabrics interact with one another? Where are the high and low values placed? Ask yourself as many questions as it takes until you understand the underpinnings of that quilt's color scheme and design. You will then know how to create your version of it even if the exact fabrics are not available.

There are many quilters who become frustrated when the exact fabrics that quilts in books and patterns are made from cannot be purchased. There are also many frustrated quilt shops that would love to provide those exact fabrics to their quilters. But the nature and time lines of the fabric industry very rarely work in cooperation of the deadlines and time lines of the publishing industry. The reality is that very few fabrics are reprinted. There are just too many new and wonderful fabrics to bring to market. To make room for them, fabrics that haven't even been around very long must be discontinued. This is why you've heard the advice to buy fabrics you love when you first see them because when they are gone — they are most likely gone forever.

In this light, taking time to understand the interaction of the fabrics in a quilt you love and want to make has some additional advantages. Once you understand what is making the quilt design work, you are free to substitute your fabric choices. In these circumstances, making the quilt becomes a wonderful creative opportunity to add yet another unique aspect to your quilt rather than feeling you are settling for second best.

Create a Library of Inspiration

Inspiration comes to us in all sorts of ways. Seldom however, does it ever make its appearance at the exact moment we summon it. Every quilter at one time has thought that the only way to decide on a color scheme is to pull the colors out of a hat. Plan to fortify your creativity with some food for thought at these times. It's much like packing yourself a survival kit of food and water, when you know that at some time or other you will be crossing the desert. Start collecting color scheme ideas as you come across them. Fabric swatches offer a bonanza of color scheme ideas. Start looking at all different kinds of fabrics, whatever you can get your hands on. Look for color combinations that particularly spark your quilt imagination. Spread out to include pictures, their subject is not important; all that matters is that you think the colors are interesting. Become an expert scavenger of color ideas and paste all of your prizes into your color journal. When the time of zero new ideas engulfs you, you will have a bounty of ideas to draw from. This color journal is a place where your creativity can regenerate itself. Then when that fabulous idea zaps you, you'll feel as though you've been singed by lightening as you run to your sewing machine.

At first glance, keeping a color journal may seem like an added complication to an already busy life. You will find that in reality, keeping this journal is very, very simple. All you will need is a 3 ring binder, a glue stick and a trip to the copy machine. On page 141 you will find a page specifically designed for your color journal with permission to make copies (for your personal use only). Use this page to paste your swatches on. You will notice that it includes a place to note the color scheme of your swatch as well as a place to record your quilt ideas that the colors have inspired.

A Quickie Review of Quilt Design Basics

To a quilt maniac few things can equal the fun of quilting. As you start your creative journey, use this list of basic design principles as a mental checklist, but most importantly … Enjoy … Enjoy … Enjoy!

- Consciously work to create harmony of color, pattern and design by using contrasts based on differences and building unifying relationships based on common elements. (Resolve to keep matching to a minimum.)

- Choose a dominant color; it can be represented by many variations of value and intensity of that color family. As you work with color, don't forget that color is either influencing or being influenced by other colors around it — make that work to your advantage.

- Use an interesting arrangement of values. Value is a key ingredient of how the eye will travel over the entire quilt design. It has a huge influence on the overall look of your quilt.

- Vary the proportions of color as well as other design elements. Equal proportions of any element make for a static design. Varying the proportions of color and print elements will give your quilt energy and movement.

- Experiment, experiment, experiment. Only through hands-on experience will you become skilled at using fabrics to create the quilts you love. Give yourself the luxury and freedom to try out your color and print ideas before committing yourself to a whole quilt. Use the personal design board for the indispensable design tool that it is.

- Always evaluate all of your decisions with the Rule of 6 Feet. Remember that your artist's eye knows more about your inner vision than anyone else. Listen to your inner voice.

A quilt is a marriage of color and texture, of love and inspiration. Put everything you have learned about color and design to use as you start your next quilt. Learn to listen to the artist within and have faith in your choices. With knowledge and by following your intuition you will grow as a quiltmaker and love the quilts you make.

The
Quilt Gallery

A Few Rules of the Road ...

As you feast your eyes on this special collection
of quilt designs, don't let that bossy little voice inside of
your head tell you what you can and cannot do.
Remember that easy quilts don't always look simplistic
and quilts that look intricate are not necessarily
challenging — the secret lies in how the quilt is put
together.

Don't limit yourself by defining what on the surface
looks to be hard or easy. Rather, find a quilt you love and
just go for it! If you follow the instructions one step at a
time, just like eating that proverbial elephant, you will
end up with a beautiful quilt plus you may even be a
little amazed at what you have accomplished.

So let's get started and
Enjoy ... Enjoy ... Enjoy!

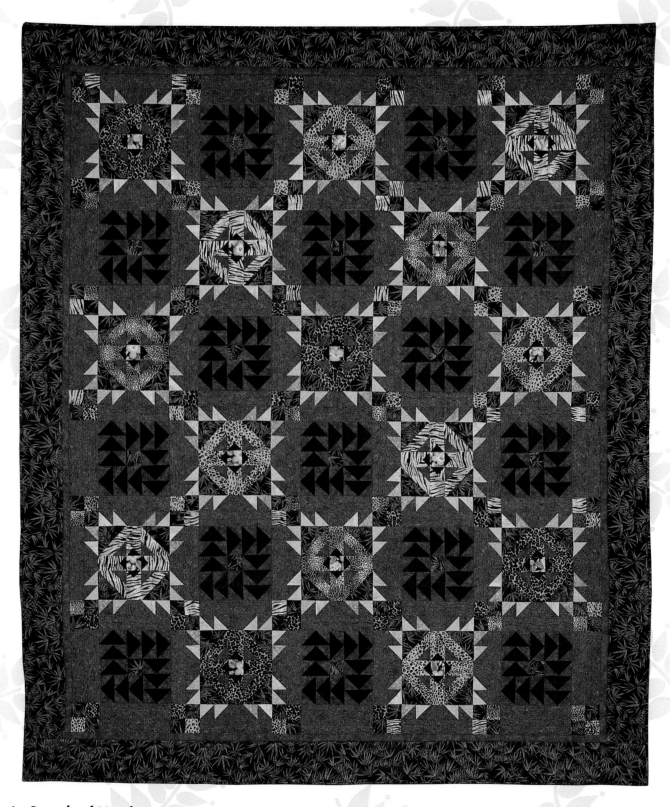

In Search of Hemingway
Approximate size: 87" x 101"
Made by: Nicole Chambers
Quilted by: Grumpy

If you have the heart of an adventurer and an eye for the dramatic or have been wondering how to use all those fabulous animal prints you've been collecting — making this quilt is almost as much fun as going on Safari. Instructions on page 92.

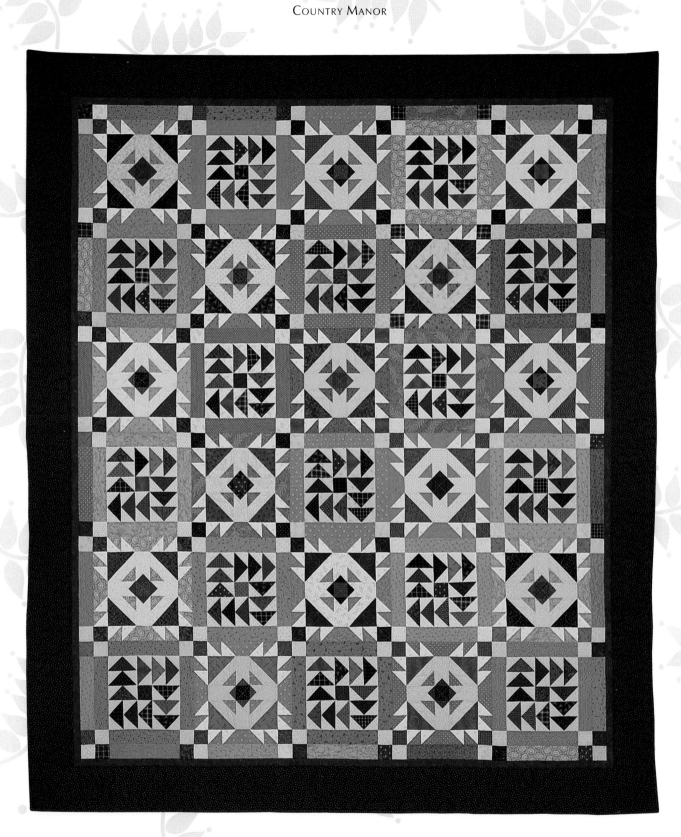

Country Manor

Approximate size: 87" x 101"
Made by: Linda Peck
Quilted by: Merline McLaughlin

If your tastes run towards less drama and more to the comfort and charm of softer traditional color choices — this color variation of *In Search of Hemingway* is a fun scrappy quilt to make. It's interesting to see how different fabrics can change the whole personality of a quilt. Instructions on page 94.

Water Wheel

Approximate size: 64" x 74"
Made by: Nicole Chambers
Quilted by: Marilyn Badger

The simple construction technique of this quilt belie its many possibili-ties. Definitely in the quickie category, this quilt is both fast and very easy. Make it fun and casual or elegant and sophisticated — it's all in the fabrics you choose. Instructions on page 73.

Moonlight Serenade

Approximate size: 88" x 104"
Made by: Nicole Chambers
Quilted by: Grumpy

Inspired by a moonlit garden, this quilt lends itself to many, many fabric possibilities. Based on two very easy blocks, it whips together in no time (but then again you don't need to feel obligated to share that thought). Instructions on page 68.

Daydreams

Approximate size: 88" x 108"
Made by: Nicole Chambers
Quilted by: Grumpy

This quilt offers you a wonderful opportunity to experiment with many fabrics without the color placement strategy getting too complex or challenging. The strong diagonal lines of the quilt will make your color choices stand out while the large background area gives you a place to show off your prints. Instructions on page 108.

The Bounty of Harvest

Approximate size: 48" x 19"
Made by: Nicole Chambers

Stripes offer many quilt designs an added element of movement and interest. Experiment a little with this table runner. Using stripes in this design is fun and easy. Instructions on page 127. ▼

Homemade Pie

Approximate size: 46" x 21"
Made by: Nicole Chambers

This table runner speaks of picnics and oooh ... those delicious pies, all things we associate with the joys of summer. A great way to use your fruit and vegetable prints. Instructions on page 125.

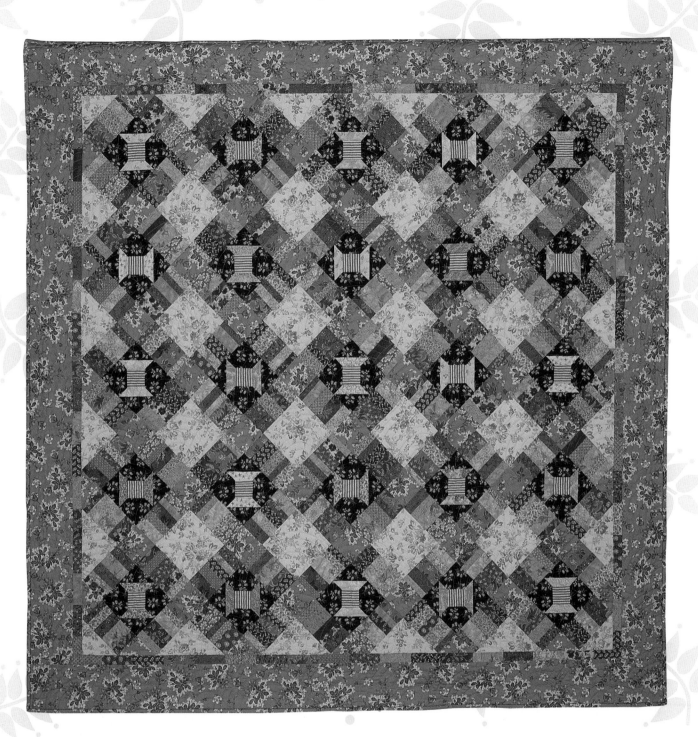

Spools

Approximate size: 73" x 73"
Made by: Nicole Chambers
Quilted by: Marilyn Badger

Make yourself a "quilt scrapbook" of all the quilts you've made and given away. This design is a great way to show off those quilt scraps or use bits and pieces of your pet fabrics (they'll be easy to admire). The threaded spool construction is easy but if you are looking for a complete no brainer, instructions are also included for super easy empty spools. Instructions on page 87.

French Bread

Approximate size: 51" x 18"
Made by: Nicole Chambers

The strong graphic design of the stars provide the perfect opportunity to showcase fabric that would otherwise lose its charm when cut into small pieces. This table runner is a terrific way to enjoy those fabrics. Instructions on page 131. ▼

Celebrate the Seasons

Approximate size: 38" x 16"
Made by: Nicole Chambers

Bright and happy in spring colors, this design lends itself easily to many other themes and seasons. Make a special table runner to usher in each season with style. Instructions on page 129.

Tutti Frutti
Approximate size: 38" x 16"
Made by: Nicole Chambers
▼

You won't have to think too long to see the many possibilities this table runner or wall hanging has to offer. Make it whimsical and fun — or perhaps something a little more serious for the den or office. Or consider adding a few blocks to make a very cute quilt for baby. Instructions on page 134.

Snow Princess
Approximate size:
42" x 18"
Made by:
Nicole Chambers
▼

The strong contrasting colors add much impact to this snowflake design. This project whips together 1-2-3 into a stunning table runner but don't overlook the design potential of making a bigger quilt. Instructions on page 137.

Times Remembered

Approximate size: 88" x 106"
Made by: Nicole Chambers
Quilted by: Kimberly Olerich

This quilt was designed in honor of Grandma Dot who LOVED blue (so much so that we used to have great fun teasing her). Even though only blue and white is used, notice the interesting effect the combination of geometric and floral prints create. The pieced border is one of the easiest borders you'll ever make. Instructions on page 112.

Celestial Waltz

Approximate size: 84" x 104"
Made by: Jane Wise
Quilted by: Marilyn Badger

If you've never made a scrappy quilt before, this quilt is an excellent place to start. The design is a combination of organized colors sprinkled with a generous assortment of scrappy fabrics that will look great no matter where they end up. You'll have so much fun, you'll be wondering why it took you so long to try scrappy! Instructions on page 76.

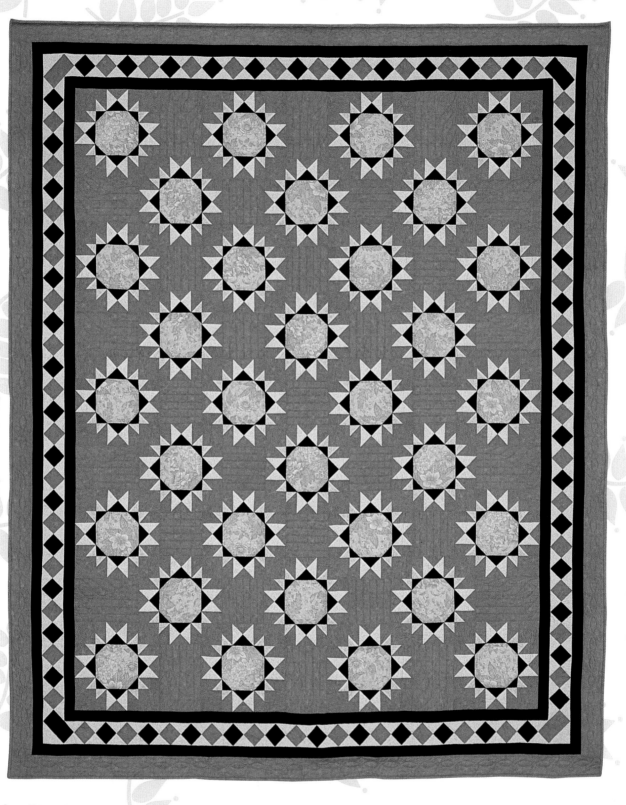

Baker Street

Approximate size: 84" x 102"
Made by: Pat Chittenden
Quilted by: Grumpy

You could make 10 quilts using this design and each one would look dramatically different. The center of the block offer a wonderful area to showcase large scale prints or specialty fabrics. Then again, you could make it in neutrals as shown here to show off the strong graphic statement this quilt makes. Instructions on page 103.

Intrigue on the Orient Express

Approximate size: 87" x 104"
Made by: Nicole Chambers
Quilted by: Grumpy

It's fun to combine the traditional with the exotic. The blocks and border are fun to make while the plain fabric squares give you wonderful areas to show off the quilting. When you need to make a beautiful quilt — fast, or you have that special fabric you want to show off, this design offers many possibilities. Instructions on page 116.

Water Lilies

Approximate size: 92" x 116"
Made by: Nicole Chambers
Quilted by: Marilyn Badger

You may be amazed at the ease with which *Water Lilies* comes together. It's made up entirely of 16" blocks that are set on point so it shouldn't surprise you to discover that it goes together pretty fast as well. Whoever said you had to suffer for your art obviously didn't know about this quilt design. Instructions on page 82.

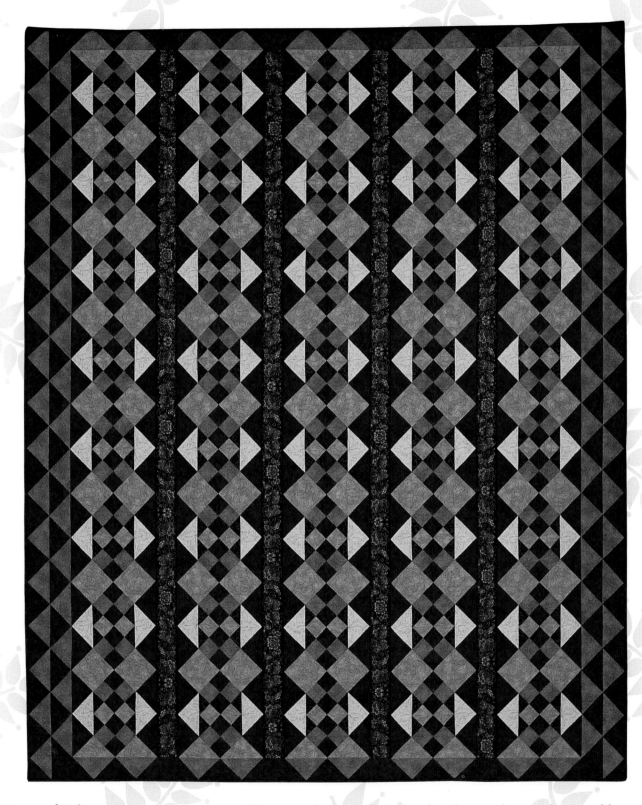

Days of Wine & Roses
Approximate size: 84" x 102"
Made by: Nicole Chambers
Quilted by: Marilyn Badger

You can make this quilt look soft and romantic or go for something strong and dramatic. This design is deceptively easy so don't let the construction technique worry you. If you've been admiring those beautiful border stripes and have been wondering how to use them, this quilt offers many possibilities. Instructions on page 98.

What a Wonderful Day!

Approximate Size: 59" x 68"
Made by: Nicole Chambers
Quilted by: Donna Larson

The simple construction techniques used in this quilt makes the interlocking pinwheels almost foolproof. Bright colors give this quilt energy but the design lends itself to a softer look as well. Instructions on page 121.

Step-by-Step
Instructions

Shortcuts
& Other Important Stuff

Yipppeeeee!
NO More Sewing Lines to Draw

Marking diagonal sewing lines on fabric squares and rectangles can become tedious, not to mention boring. Do yourself a favor — run, don't walk to your favorite quilt shop and get yourself The Angler2™. For an investment of a few dollars, you will save countless hours and have the luxury of never having to draw another sewing line again (well, almost never).

As an added bonus, The Angler2™ is marked with a scant $1/4$" seam allowance that is very accurate, so achieving that sometimes elusive $1/4$ inch seam allowance becomes a piece of cake. Next to my rotary cutters and rulers, this is one of my favorite sewing tools. There are no less than 2 in my sewing studio at all times (a girl's got to have a backup).

You can also make your own seam guide. On a piece of graph paper (approximately 3" x 5") mark the guide line lengthwise in the middle of the paper. Place this paper on your machine and lower the needle (about 1" from the top end) into the line you've drawn. Lower the presser foot. Lay a ruler (preferably one with an $1/8$" grid) against the side edge of your presser foot. Use the grid of the ruler to square up the grid of the graph paper. When you are sure your guide line is absolutely straight, secure the bottom end of your guide with tape. Cut enough off of the top end so that your feed dogs are free and the paper is not in your way.

If you don't like having a paper guide taped to your machine, you can also mark the guide by using a piece of masking tape or place the mark directly onto your machine with a permanent marker. Just be sure the guide line you are using is straight.

You can now use this guide to line up your pieces corner to corner, sewing a perfect diagonal seam without having to mark each individual piece. ❤

Make a Multitude of Half Square Triangles ... FAST

When you need a fairly large number of half square triangles, you may want to consider making them by using the grid method. It's a fast and reliable way to make many half square triangles at one time. In my opinion, the best alternative (as in easiest and fastest ... leaving more time to quilt) is to use commercially produced preprinted grids such as Triangle Paper™ rather than drawing the grid yourself.

But whether you decide to draw your own grid or use one already printed for you, the secret to getting accurate half square triangles is by sewing accurately on the sewing lines and cutting accurately on the cutting lines. If you find this particularly difficult, you may want to consider making larger half square triangles than what you actually need and cutting them down to size.

So whether you are a Do-It-Yourselfer or you need a multitude of half square triangles in a size that is not commercially available, follow the simple instructions described below to draw your own grid.

Prepare your fabric by pressing the right sides of the 2 fabrics together using an iron. You may want to treat the fabrics with spray sizing to give them a little extra body and make them easier to work with. To keep things manageable, don't plan on using fabric pieces larger than 18″ x 20″ and remember to leave enough space for a margin on all the four edges.

For best results use a fine tip permanent fabric pen and mark on the wrong side of the lighter fabric.

Using the fabric pen and a ruler, mark a grid of squares as illustrated. The size of squares you will need to draw will be the same size that is specified in the instructions. For instance, if the instructions ask you to cut (20) $2^7/8''$ squares (of two fabrics), you know that you will need to draw 20 squares and that they need to be $2^7/8''$ in size.

Next, draw diagonal lines through each square on the grid, again refer to the illustration. With a $^1/4$ inch presser foot, sew along each side of all diagonal lines. (Each side is sewn in one continuous seam.)

Press stitched fabric. Using a rotary cutter and a ruler, cut all squares apart. Then cut squares in half in-between the diagonal stitching lines. Gently press triangle squares open, pressing seam allowance towards the dark fabric. Trim off dog ears. Remember, accuracy in marking, sewing and cutting is crucial to making your half square triangles come out the perfect size. ❤

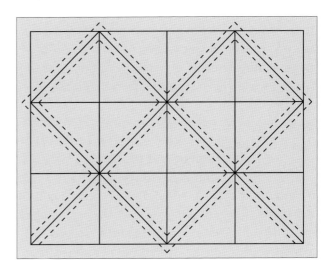

Quilting is as Easy as 1-2-3

The longer you quilt, the more "tricks" you'll learn and have up your sleeve. But ultimately all of the tricks in the world won't give you the beautiful results you want if you don't follow the 3 Golden Rules of Quilting. Following these guidelines will give you consistently sized blocks, seams that match, in other words — quilting projects that are fun to work on and quilts you are proud to show off!

1. Cut Accurately

Always take a few seconds to make sure you are measuring and cutting your fabric to the exact size specified and that your pieces are in-square. You would be amazed how many quilter think close enough is OK and then wonder why their blocks don't fit together very well and their points don't match up. How accurately you've cut your pieces is the foundation of how the entire quilt will go together so be assured that your efforts in this area are really going to count.

Check whether the blade in your rotary cutter is still sharp before you start cutting out your quilt. It's easy to lose track of the last time you replaced the blade and you know what happens when you try to slice of loaf of bread with a dulled knife — you don't want to do that to your beautiful fabric.

Before you start cutting strips, square up your fabric edge and then remember to re-square it after every 3 or 4 cuts (follow this step when you are re-cutting your strips into squares and rectangles as well).

2. Sew Accurately

Make sure your seam allowance is consistently a scant $^1/4$ inch. Double check yourself every once in a while by sewing 4 strips ($1^1/2''$ x $4^1/2''$) together. Press seams to one side and measure. You should have a $4^1/2''$ x $4^1/2''$ square.

Thread is not the place to skimp. Use a good quality neutral colored thread and replace your sewing machine needle frequently to maintain high quality stitches.

3. Press Gently

More potentially perfect blocks get pushed and shoved out of shape at the ironing board than any-where else. For some reason the ironing board seems to unleash a lot of pent up emotion from even the most genteel quilters. Don't use a heavy hand or strong back and forth movements. That style of ironing will simply spell disaster for your quilt. Remind yourself to press GENTLY (yet firmly) with up and down movements. With a good quality iron, this technique will get the job done nicely.

My preference is to use a really hot iron with a little steam. Be sure to give your pressed pieces a chance to cool before moving them to further insure against pulling them out of shape. Take extra care to be gentle when you are pressing pieces with raw bias edges. ❤

To Wash or Not to Wash
... that is the Question

To wash or not to wash fabric before making a quilt is a debate that has been going on since the beginning of time. And still a consensus has not been reached — probably because there just aren't any clear and easy answers. Each side has its benefits and drawbacks. Fabric straight off of the bolt has wonderful body, plus you have the added advantage to getting right down to the business of quilting!

Pre-washing on the other hand means you have given yourself the assurance that the fabrics won't shrink and that they are colorfast. You now have the luxury of quilting with an easy mind. However, it does mean that you have to do laundry before you can quilt with any fabric that hasn't been washed.

These days, you can feel fairly secure that most quality quilting fabrics are for the most part colorfast. In my opinion it never hurts to play it safe and test reds, burgundies, turquoises, blues, purples — you know, the troublemakers.

What has cropped up as a potential reason to rethink the pre-washing issue once again is the problem of shrinking. Cotton fabrics have been shrinking a little since ... forever, so what is the big deal?

Recently, it's been my experience that the shrinking has been significantly uneven, much more in the width of the fabric than in the length. This shrinking has occurred under the most common situations such as using a little steam or spritzing a fabric square with a little water to get out a stubborn crease.

Some fabrics that go to the ironing board completely square come back a little rectangular as well as smaller. This can be annoying.

In most instances, this issue has been enough to motivated me to pre-wash. If you find yourself having that Twilight Zone feeling when your pieces are slightly out of square even though you know you've cut them perfectly and you've been very careful while pressing them, uneven shrinking may be the culprit.

If you do decide to pre-wash, use a mild soap, cool water and unfold all of the fabric before putting it into the washing machine. Don't overdry the fabric in the dryer. Press the fabric from the wrong side while using a generous amount of spray sizing to give the fabric that *off the bolt* feeling. It is also a good idea to buy a little extra fabric to make up for any shrinking that may occur. ❤

DESIGNER TIP: The Secret of Cutting Geometric Fabrics on Grain

Geometric prints look fabulous in quilts but sometimes they can be real pickles to cut. If you are a quilter who doesn't like geometric prints to be cut off kilter, this technique works wonders when you are working with fabrics that have an obvious geometric pattern. To keep your pieces from being cut topsy turvey, follow this simple procedure.

Instead of cutting strips across the width of the fabric as you normally would, cut a 21″ section off of your yardage. Make sure selvages are absolutely even. Trim off selvages by lining up your ruler evenly against the printed design. Cut your strips as you normally would from this edge, occasionally re-squaring your fabric so that your strips are cutting straight with the print. If the print is particularly off grain, cut strips from a single layer.

When you need longer strips, cut a 42″ section off of your yardage. Unfold fabric, pressing out the center crease. Refold fabric so selvages are now at the top and bottom of your piece of fabric and perfectly even. Trim off selvages as before and cut your strips.

❤

FABRIC CHART

Let your quilt imagination inspire you as you choose fabrics that reflect your unique interpretation of the quilt design.

You will notice that fabric colors are only listed in the fabric requirements. After that they are simply referred to as fabric A, B, C, etc. This is purposefully done to not unduly influence your creativity as you plan YOUR fabric choices and also to keep you from having to constantly remind yourself what colors you've substituted.

Use this chart as a handy reference to keep track of your fabric choices while you sew — and have fun, fun, fun.

Permission granted to make copies of this page. For personal use only.

Fabric A

Fabric B

Fabric C

Fabric D

Fabric E

Fabric F

Fabric G

Fabric H

Fabric I

Moonlight Serenade *approximate size 88" x 104"*

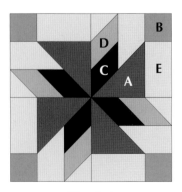

Block A

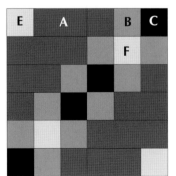

Block B

Fabric Requirements: *color photo on page 42 & 50*

Fabric A *(Dark blue floral)*	$6^3/4$* yards
Fabric B *(Green)*	$2^1/4$
Fabric C *(Burgundy)*	$1^1/2$
Fabric D *(Dark pink)*	$7/8$
Fabric E *(Beige floral)*	$2^5/8$
Fabric F *(Medium pink)*	$1/2$

*includes binding

Cutting Instructions for Moonlight Serenade

Block A

Fabric A
10 strips $4^1/2$" wide   Cut into (80) $4^1/2$" squares

Fabric B
5 strips $2^1/2$" wide

Fabric C
5 strips $4^1/2$" wide   Cut into (80) $2^1/2$" x $4^1/2$" rectangles

---

Fabric D
5 strips $4^1/2$" wide   Cut into (80) $2^1/2$" x $4^1/2$" rectangles

---

Fabric E
5 strips $6^1/2$" wide   Cut into (80) $2^1/2$" x $6^1/2$" rectangles
5 strips $4^1/2$" wide
5 strips $2^1/2$" wide   Cut into (80) $2^1/2$" squares

Block B

Fabric A
8 strips $2^1/2$" wide
7 strips $4^1/2$" wide
5 strips $6^1/2$" wide   Cut into (48) $2^1/2$" x $6^1/2$" rectangles *and*
                                                 (12) $4^1/2$" x $6^1/2$" rectangles

Setting triangles
3 strips $16^3/4$" wide   Cut into (5) $16^3/4$" squares cut in half diagonally twice *and*
                                                 (2) $10^3/4$" squares cut in half once *(corner triangles)*
6 strips $2^1/2$" wide   Cut into (18) $12^1/4$" lengths

Binding
10 strips $2^1/2$" wide

Fabric B
22 strips $2^1/2$" wide   Cut into (18) $2^1/2$" squares
                                         leave 20 strips whole

---

Fabric C
8 strips $2^1/2$" wide

Fabric E
3 strips $2^1/2$" wide

Fabric F
4 strips $2^1/2$" wide

Sewing Instructions

Block A

On the wrong side of fabric D $2^1/2$" x $4^1/2$" rectangles, draw a hatch mark $2^1/2$" from the top. Simply place 2 rectangles at right angles to each other matching the top edge and mark as illustrated in Figure 1.

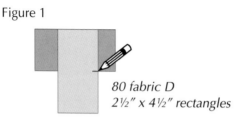

Figure 1

80 fabric D
$2^1/2$" x $4^1/2$" rectangles

Draw a diagonal line from the outer corner to this mark as illustrated in Figure 2 *(see shortcuts)*.

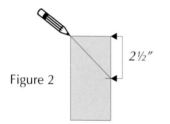

Figure 2

$2^1/2$"

Layer fabric C and D $2^1/2$" x $4^1/2$" rectangles right sides together as illustrated in Figure 3. Sew on the pencil line. Trim seam allowance to $1/4$" and press seam as arrow indicates.

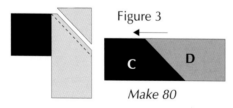

Figure 3

C   D

Make 80

Sew this pieced section and a fabric E $2^1/2$" x $6^1/2$" rectangle together as illustrated in Figure 4. Press seam as arrow indicates.

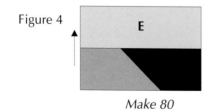

Figure 4

E

Make 80

Using a sharp pencil, draw a diagonal line on the wrong side of 80 fabric A $4^1/2$" squares and fabric E $2^1/2$" squares *(see shortcuts)*.

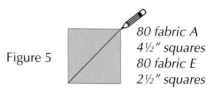

Figure 5

80 fabric A
$4^1/2$" squares
80 fabric E
$2^1/2$" squares

With right sides together, position a fabric A $4^1/2$" square on the pieced section as illustrated in Figure 6. Stitch on the pencil line. Cut seam allowance to $1/4$" and press towards outer edge.

Figure 6

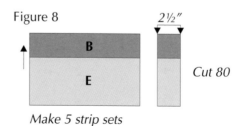

A

Make 80

Repeat these steps, this time using a fabric E $2^1/2$" square. Place as illustrated in Figure 7.

Figure 7

E

Make 80

Sew a fabric E $4^1/2$" strip and a fabric B $2^1/2$" strip together lengthwise. Press seam as arrow indicates. Cutting across the pieced strip set, cut into $2^1/2$" sections.

Figure 8

B

E

$2^1/2$"

Cut 80

Make 5 strip sets

Sew onto pieced unit as illustrated in Figure 9. Press seam as arrow indicates.

Figure 9

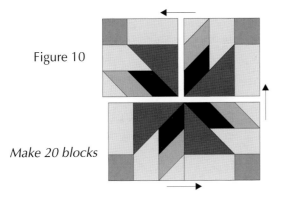

Refer to Figure 10 and sew units together to form block. Press seams as arrows indicate.

Figure 10

Make 20 blocks

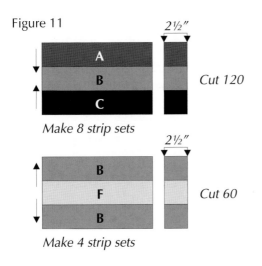

Block B

Refer to Figure 11 and sew indicated 2½" and 4½" strips together lengthwise. Press seams as arrows indicate. Cutting across the pieced strip sets cut into 2½" sections.

Figure 11

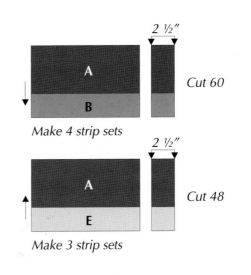

2 ½"

A
B
Cut 60

Make 4 strip sets

2 ½"

A
E
Cut 48

Make 3 strip sets

❤

IMPORTANT NOTE: *As you are working on block B, be sure to match the orientation of your units to those pictured in the illustrations. It will have an important impact on the direction of the seams in your block as well as giving you the best seam butting strategy.*

Make a 9-patch checkerboard by sewing strip sets together as illustrated in Figure 12. Press seams as arrows indicate.

Figure 12

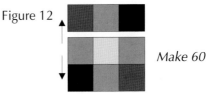

Make 60

Refer to Figure 13 and sew remaining strip sets and fabric A (2½" x 6½" and 4½" x 6½") rectangles together. Press seams as arrows indicate.

Figure 13

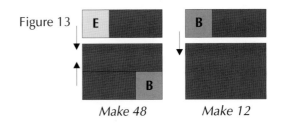

Make 48   Make 12

2½"

A
B
C
Cut 120

Make 8 strip sets

2½"

B
F
B
Cut 60

Make 4 strip sets

Sew units together to form blocks as illustrated in Figure 14. Press seams as arrows indicate.

Figure 14

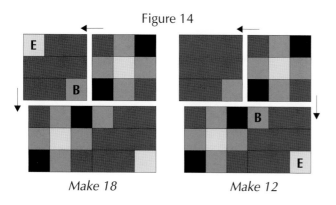

Make 18   Make 12

Setting Triangles

Sew a fabric B 2¹/₂" square onto one end of 18 fabric A 2¹/₂" x 12¹/₄" strips. Press seam as arrow indicates.

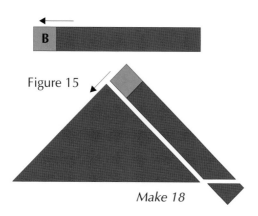

Figure 15

Make 18

Sew this unit onto side of setting triangle as illustrated in Figure 15 and press. Using a ruler and rotary cutter, trim off excess fabric so triangle edge is even.

Sew blocks, setting triangles and corner triangles together as diagrammed in Figure 16. Make 2 of each row.

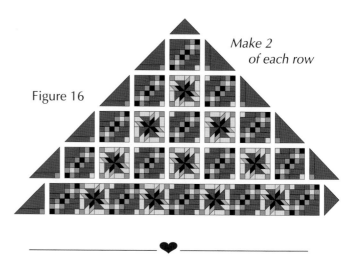

Make 2 of each row

Figure 16

HINT: *Handle and press patchwork with care. Since blocks are set on point, the patchwork is vulnerable to being stretched out of shape until it is quilted.*

Sew rows together as illustrated in Figure 17 and press. Sew quilt halves together. If necessary, trim setting triangles so quilt edge is even.

Figure 17

Water Wheel *approximate size 64" x 74"*

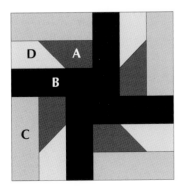

Block A

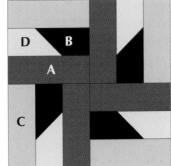

Block B

Fabric Requirements: *color photo on page 26 & 49*

Fabric A *(Red print)*	2¹/₂* yards
Fabric B *(Black print)*	2¹/₈
Fabric C *(Taupe print)*	1¹/₂
Fabric D *(Light beige)*	1¹/₈

*includes binding

Cutting Instructions for Water Wheel

Fabric A

| 5 strips | 5" wide | Cut into (84) 5" x 2" rectangles |
| 5 strips | 3¹/₂" wide | Cut into (84) 3¹/₂" x 2" rectangles |

Outer Border

| 7 strips | 2" wide | |

Binding

| 8 strips | 2¹/₂" wide | |

Fabric B

| 5 strips | 5" wide | Cut into (84) 5" x 2" rectangles |
| 5 strips | 3¹/₂" wide | Cut into (84) 3¹/₂" x 2" rectangles |

Inner Border

| 6 strips | 3¹/₂" wide | |

Fabric C

| 9 strips | 5" wide | Cut into (168) 5" x 2" rectangles |

Fabric D

| 9 strips | 3¹/₂" wide | Cut into (168) 3¹/₂" x 2" rectangles |

Sewing Instructions

On the wrong side of fabric D 2" x 3¹/₂" rectangles, draw a hatch mark 2" from the top. Simply place 2 rectangles at right angles to each other matching the top edge and mark as illustrated in Figure 1.

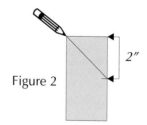

Figure 2

Figure 1

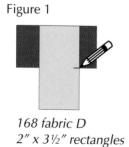

168 fabric D
2" x 3½" rectangles

Layer 2" x 3¹/₂" rectangles right sides together as illustrated in Figure 3. Sew on the pencil line. Trim seam allowance to ¹/₄" and press seams towards the darker fabric.

Figure 3

Draw a diagonal line from the outer corner to this hatch mark as illustrated in Figure 2 *(see shortcuts)*.

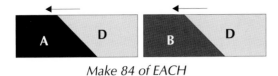

Make 84 of EACH

Sew pieced sections and 2" x 5" rectangles together as illustrated in Figure 4. Press seams as arrows indicate.

Figure 4

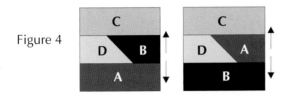

Make 84 of EACH

Sew matching units together to form blocks as illustrated in Figure 5. Press seams as arrows indicate. Make 21 of each block.

Figure 5

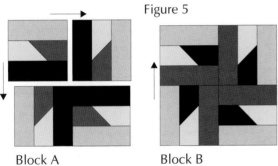

Block A   Block B

Make 21 of EACH block

Sew 6 alternating blocks A and B together to form a row. Press seams in one direction.

———————————— ♥ ————————————

HINT: *As you are sewing the blocks together, be sure the center seams are falling in opposite directions. This will insure that all remaining seams will butt together.*

Figure 6

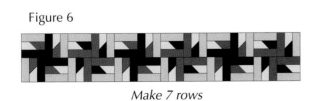

Make 7 rows

Sew rows together making sure blocks A and B are alternating. Press seams in one direction.

Figure 7

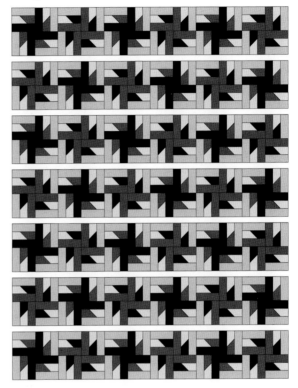

Measure the length of your quilt *(through the center of the quilt)* and piece 2 fabric B border strips (3$\frac{1}{2}$") to that measurement. Sew to each side of the quilt and press seams towards outer edge.

Apply border to top and bottom of the quilt using the same technique.

Repeat these steps for the second border using fabric A strips (2").

Celestial Waltz approximate size 84" x 104"

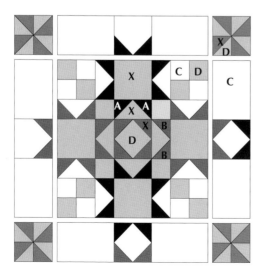

Fabric Requirements: *color photo on page 8 & 57*

Fabric A *(Purple floral)*	$3^1/2$ yards
Fabric B *(Green print)*	$2^1/2$*
Fabric C *(White)*	$4^1/2$
Fabric D *(Yellow floral)*	$2^3/8$
Fabric X *(Assorted prints)*	14 fat quarters

* includes binding

Cutting Instructions for Celestial Waltz

Fabric A

12 strips	$2^1/2$" wide	Cut into (192) $2^1/2$" squares

Border

14 strips	$4^1/2$" wide	Cut into (18) $4^1/2$" x $6^1/2$" rectangles *and* (18) $4^1/2$" x $16^1/2$" rectangles leave 3 strips whole
3 strips	$2^1/2$" wide	Cut into (8) $2^1/2$" squares leave 2 strips whole

---

Fabric B

12 strips	$2^1/2$" wide	Cut into (192) $2^1/2$" squares

Outer Border

10 strips	$2^1/2$" wide

Binding

10 strips	2 $1/2$" wide

Fabric C

8 strips	$6^1/2$" wide	Cut into (62) $4^1/2$" x $6^1/2$" rectangles
10 strips	$4^1/2$" wide	Cut into (31) $4^1/2$" squares *and* (96) $2^1/2$" x $4^1/2$" rectangles
6 strips	$2^1/2$" wide	

Border

2 strips	$6^1/2$" wide	Cut into (14) $4^1/2$" x $6^1/2$" rectangles
2 strips	$4^1/2$" wide	
2 strips	$2^1/2$" wide	

Fabric D

2 strips	$4^1/2$" wide	Cut into (12) $4^1/2$" squares
◣ 7 strips	$2^7/8$" wide	Cut into (76) $2^7/8$" squares
10 strips	$2^1/2$" wide	Cut into (52) $2^1/2$" squares leave 6 strips whole

Border

7 strips	$2^1/2$" wide

Fabric X *(Assorted fabrics)*
Cut along the wide edge of fat quarters

12 strips	$4^1/2$" wide	Cut into (48) $4^1/2$" squares
6 strips	$4^1/2$" wide	Cut into (48) $2^1/2$" x $4^1/2$" rectangles – ***in matching sets of 4***
6 strips	$2^1/2$" wide	Cut into (48) $2^1/2$" squares – ***in matching sets of 4***
◣ 13 strips	$2^7/8$" wide	Cut into (76) $2^7/8$" squares – ***in matching sets of 2***

◣ Do NOT cut these strips if you plan on making half square triangles by drawing a grid or using products such as Triangle Paper™

Sewing Instructions

Section 1

Draw a diagonal line on the wrong side of all fabric A, B and X 2½" squares (see shortcuts).

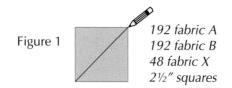

Figure 1

192 fabric A
192 fabric B
48 fabric X
2½" squares

With right sides together, position a 2½" square on the corner of a 2½" x 4½" rectangle. Stitch on the pencil line. Cut seam allowance to ¼" and press seam towards outer edge. Repeat these steps for the other corner. Refer to Figure 2.

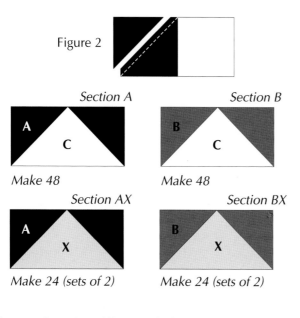

Figure 2

Section A
A C
Make 48

Section B
B C
Make 48

Section AX
A X
Make 24 (sets of 2)

Section BX
B X
Make 24 (sets of 2)

Sew sections A and B to each side of a fabric X 4½" square. Press seams as arrows indicate.

Figure 3

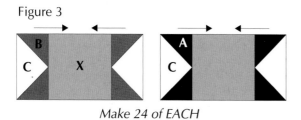

B C X

A C

Make 24 of EACH

Section 2

Starting at one corner, with right sides together, place a 2½" square on top of a 4½" square. Stitch on the pencil line. Refer to Figure 4 for color designations. Cut seam allowance to ¼" and press towards outer edge.

Figure 4

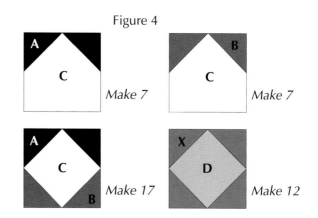

A C   Make 7

B C   Make 7

A C B   Make 17

X D   Make 12

Sew a *matching* set of sections AX to each side of section 2 (fabric D/X) as illustrated in Figure 5. Press seams as arrows indicate.

Figure 5

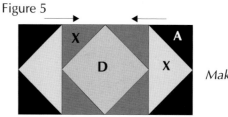

X D A X   Make 12

Sew a fabric D 2½" square onto each end of the remaining sections BX. Press seams as arrows indicate.

Figure 6

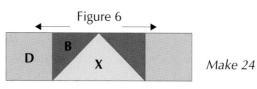

D B X   Make 24

Sew sections together as illustrated in Figure 7. **Make sure the indicated fabric X sections match.** Press seams as arrows indicate.

Figure 7

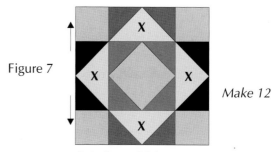

X X X X   Make 12

Match indicated fabric X sections

Section 3

Sew fabric C and D 2¹/₂" strips together lengthwise. Press seam towards darker fabric. Cutting across the pieced strip, cut 96 pieces 2¹/₂" long.

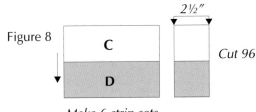

Figure 8

2¹/₂"

C

D

Cut 96

Make 6 strip sets

Make a 4-patch checkerboard by sewing 2 sections together as illustrated.

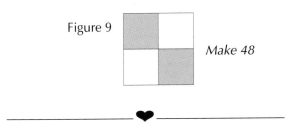

Figure 9

Make 48

---❤---

HINT: *To achieve a nicely joined seam intersection, nestle intersecting seams together before sewing. Do NOT place a pin at the intersecting point.*

Arrange sections as illustrated in Figure 10. **Pay special attention to the color layout.** Sew sections into 3 horizontal rows. Press seams as arrows indicate.

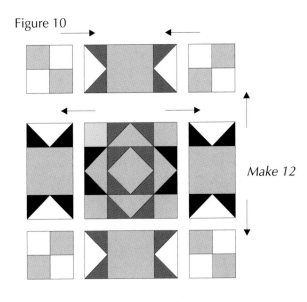

Figure 10

Make 12

Sew rows together to form block.

Pinwheels

Use your favorite technique to make half square triangles *(see shortcuts)* or use the following method.

Place fabric D and X 2⁷/₈" squares right sides together. Cut them in half diagonally. Sew triangles together on the wide edge. Press seam towards darker fabric and trim off dog ears. Handle bias edges carefully when you are sewing them together.

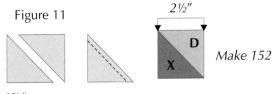

Figure 11

2¹/₂"

D

X

Make 152

2⁷/₈" squares
fabrics D and X

Sew half square triangles together to make pinwheels as illustrated in Figure 12.

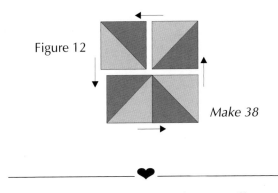

Figure 12

Make 38

---❤---

HINT: *Undo several stitches in the seam allowance of the pinwheel center and press seams in the direction the arrows in Figure 12 indicate.*

Section 4

Sew a fabric C 4¹/₂" x 6¹/₂" rectangle onto each end of sections 2 as illustrated in Figure 13. Press seams as arrows indicate.

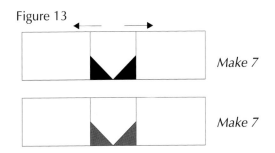

Figure 13

Make 7

Make 7

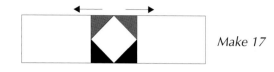

Make 17

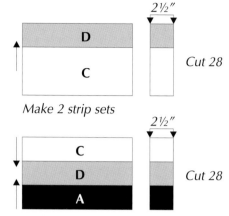

2½″

Cut 28

Make 2 strip sets

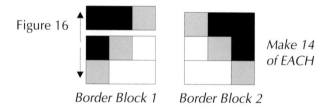

2½″

Cut 28

Make 2 strip sets

Carefully arrange pieces as illustrated in Figure 14. **Be sure all stars have matching points.** Sew sections into rows. Press seams as arrows indicate. Then sew rows together and press.

Figure 14

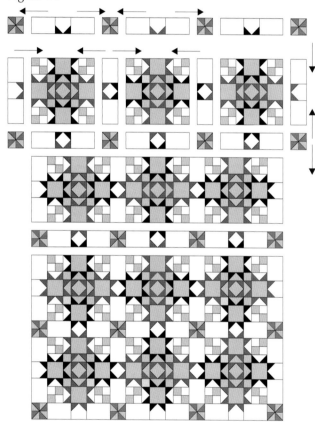

Sew border blocks together as illustrated in Figure 16. Press seams as arrows indicate.

Figure 16

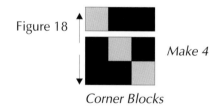

Make 14 of EACH

Border Block 1   *Border Block 2*

Sew fabric A and D 2½″ squares together. Refer to Figure 17.

Figure 17      *Make 4*

To make the corner blocks, sew sections together as illustrated in Figure 18.

Figure 18

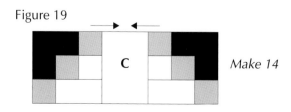

Make 4

Corner Blocks

BORDER

Sew the following 2½″ and 4½″ strips together lengthwise. Press seams as arrows indicate and cut into 2½″ sections as illustrated in Figure 15.

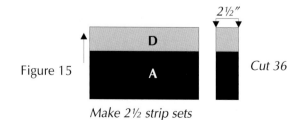

2½″

Figure 15

Cut 36

Make 2½ strip sets

Sew a fabric C 4½″ x 6½″ rectangle in-between Border Blocks 1 and 2 as illustrated in Figure 19. Press seams as arrows indicate.

Figure 19

Make 14

Sew border pieces and fabric A 4½" x 6½" rectangles together as illustrated in Figure 20. Press seams as arrows indicate.

Figure 20

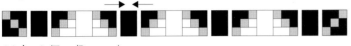

Make 2 (Top/Bottom)

Make 2 (Sides)

Sew remaining pinwheels and fabric A 4½" x 16½" rectangles together as illustrated in Figure 21. Press seams as arrows indicate.

Figure 21

Make 2 (Top/Bottom)

Make 2 (Sides)

Sew pieced border to each side of your quilt. Press seam towards outer edge. Sew pieced borders to the top and bottom of your quilt.

Apply pinwheel borders to your quilt. Press seams towards the quilt.

Outer Border

Measure the length of your quilt *(through the middle of the quilt)* and piece fabric B outer border strips (2½") to that length. Sew to each side of the quilt and press seams towards outer edge.

Using the same technique, apply the border strips to the top and bottom of your quilt.

Water Lilies *approximate size 92" x 116"*

Fabric Requirements: *color photo on page 19 & 60*

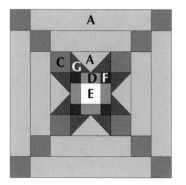

Fabric A *(Periwinkle Blue)*	4¼ yards
Fabric B *(Green/Purple print)*	5½*
Fabric C *(Light Green)*	1⅞
Fabric D *(2 Purple prints)*	
D#1	⅜
D#2	¾
Fabric E *(Yellow Batik)*	1¾
Fabric F *(Dark Purple)*	⅞
Fabric G *(Green)*	1¼

*includes binding

82

Cutting Instructions for Water Lilies

Fabric A

12 strips	4^1/$_2$" wide	Cut into (192) 2^1/$_2$" x 4^1/$_2$" rectangles
31 strips	2^1/$_2$" wide	Cut into (48) 2^1/$_2$" x 12^1/$_2$" rectangles *and*
		(48) 2^1/$_2$" x 8^1/$_2$" rectangles *and*
		(48) 2^1/$_2$" squares

Fabric B

4 strips	24" wide	Cut into (4) 24" squares cut in half diagonally twice

Cut left over fabric into (4) 24" x 12^1/$_2$" sections and then cut again into (32) 2^1/$_2$" x 12^1/$_2$" rectangles

1 strip	12^1/$_2$" wide	Cut into (2) 12^1/$_2$" squares cut in half diagonally once *(corner triangles)*
14 strips	2^1/$_2$" wide	Cut into (32) 2^1/$_2$" x 8^1/$_2$" rectangles
		leave 6 strips whole
2 strips	4^1/$_2$" wide	Cut into (32) 2^1/$_2$" x 4^1/$_2$" rectangles

Binding

11 strips	2^1/$_2$" wide

Fabric C

15 strips	2^1/$_2$" wide	Cut into (240) 2^1/$_2$" squares
12 strips	1^1/$_2$" wide	

Fabric D

2 strips *(D#1)*	4^7/$_8$" wide	Cut into (12) 4^7/$_8$" squares cut in half diagonally once
2 strips *(D#2)*	4^7/$_8$" wide	Cut into (12) 4^7/$_8$" squares cut in half diagonally once
2 strips *(D#2)*	2^1/$_2$" wide	
3 strips *(D#2)*	1^1/$_2$" wide	

Fabric E

20 strips	2^1/$_2$" wide	Cut into (288) 2^1/$_2$" squares
		leave 2 strips whole

Fabric F

2 strips	4^1/$_2$" wide	Cut into (12) 4^1/$_2$" squares
3 strips	2^1/$_2$" wide	Cut into (48) 2^1/$_2$" squares
4 strips	1^1/$_2$" wide	

Fabric G

4 strips	2^7/$_8$" wide	Cut into (48) 2^7/$_8$" squares cut in half diagonally once
10 strips	2^1/$_2$" wide	Cut into (160) 2^1/$_2$" squares

Sewing Instructions

Block A

Sew a fabric B 2¹/₂" strips and 2 fabric C 1¹/₂" strips together as illustrated in Figure 1. Press seams as arrows indicate. Cut into 4¹/₂" sections.

Figure 1

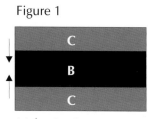

Make 6 strip sets   *Cut into 48 sections*

Draw a diagonal line on the wrong side of all fabric E 2¹/₂" squares *(see shortcuts).*

Figure 2   *288 fabric E 2¹/₂" squares*

With right sides together, position a fabric E 2¹/₂" square on the corner of a fabric A 2¹/₂" x 4¹/₂" rectangle. Stitch on the pencil line.

Cut seam allowance to ¹/₄" and press towards outer edge. Repeat these steps for the other corner. Refer to Figure 3.

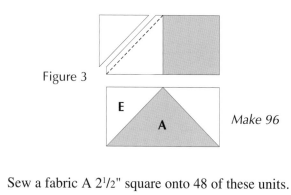

Figure 3

Make 96

Sew a fabric A 2¹/₂" square onto 48 of these units.

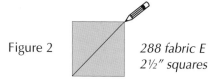

Figure 4

Make 48

Using the same techniques as before, apply fabric E 2¹/₂" squares onto the pieced sections as illustrated in Figure 5.

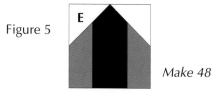

Figure 5

Make 48

Sew a fabric A 2¹/₂" x 4¹/₂" rectangle onto this unit as illustrated in Figure 6. Press as arrow indicates.

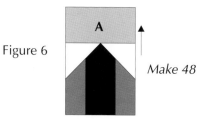

Figure 6

Make 48

Sew fabric G triangles onto fabric F 2¹/₂" square as illustrated in Figure 7. Press seams as arrows indicate.

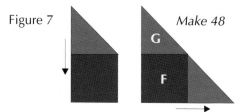

Figure 7   *Make 48*

Sew a fabric D triangle onto this unit *(make 24 units with fabric D#1 and 24 units with fabric D#2).* Press seam as arrow indicates. Refer to Figure 8.

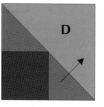

Figure 8

*Make 48
24 with fabric D#1
24 with fabric D#2*

Arrange sections as illustrated in Figure 9 and sew pieces together. Press seams as arrows indicate.

Figure 9

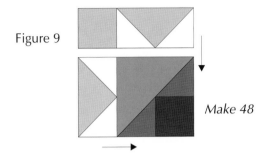

Make 48

Sew the units you've made and fabric F 4¹/2" square into horizontal rows as illustrated in Figure 10. Press seams as arrows indicate. Sew rows together to make block.

Figure 10

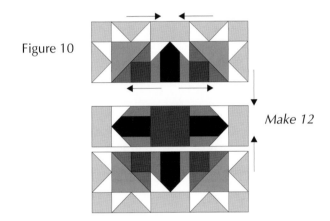

Make 12

Block B

Sew fabric E 2¹/2" strip and fabric D 1¹/2" strips together as illustrated in Figure 11. Press seams as arrows indicate. Cut into 2¹/2" sections.

Figure 11

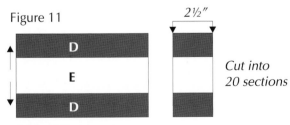

2¹/2"

Cut into 20 sections

Make 1½ strip sets

Sew fabric D 2¹/2" strip and fabric F 1¹/2" strips together as illustrated in Figure 12. Press seams as arrows indicate. Cut into 1¹/2" sections.

Figure 12

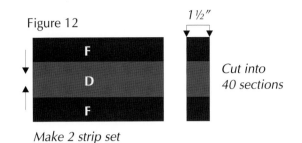

1½"

Cut into 40 sections

Make 2 strip set

Sew sections together as illustrated in Figure 13. Press seams as arrows indicate.

Figure 13

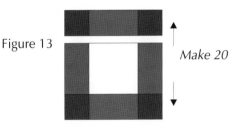

Make 20

Draw a diagonal line on the wrong side of all fabric G 2¹/2" squares *(see shortcuts)*.

Figure 14

160 fabric G 2½" squares

Using the same techniques as before, apply fabric G 2¹/2" squares onto fabric A and B 2¹/2" x 4¹/2" rectangles. Refer to Figure 15.

Figure 15

Make 48   *Make 32*

Sew these units onto each side of checkerboard as illustrated in Figure 16. Press seams as arrows indicate.

Figure 16

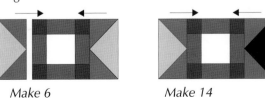

Make 6   *Make 14*

Refer to Figure 17 and apply fabric C 2$\frac{1}{2}$" squares to fabric A and B 8$\frac{1}{2}$" and 12$\frac{1}{2}$" strips as well as A/G and B/G units. Press seams as arrows indicate.

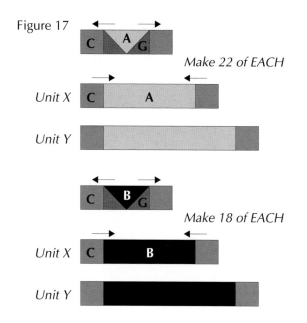

Figure 17

Make 22 of EACH

Unit X

Unit Y

Make 18 of EACH

Unit X

Unit Y

Sew units together as illustrated in Figure 18. Press seams as arrows indicate.

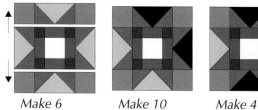

Figure 18

Make 6   Make 10   Make 4

Add 8$\frac{1}{2}$" x 2$\frac{1}{2}$" rectangles and units X to these units. Then add 12$\frac{1}{2}$" x 2$\frac{1}{2}$" rectangles and units Y. Refer to Figure 19. Press as arrows indicate after each step.

Figure 19

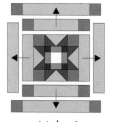 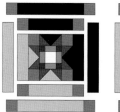

Make 6   Make 10   Make 4

Sew blocks, setting triangles and corner triangles together as diagramed in Figure 20. Make 2 of each row.

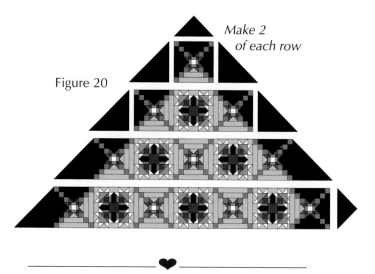

Figure 20

Make 2 of each row

HINT: Handle and press patchwork with care. Since blocks are set on point, the patchwork is vulnerable to being stretched out of shape until it is quilted.

Sew rows together as illustrated in Figure 21. You will have 2 quilt halves. Sew quilt halves together. If necessary, trim setting triangles so quilt edge is even.

Figure 21

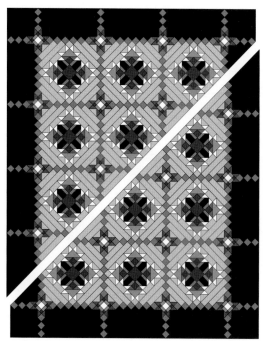

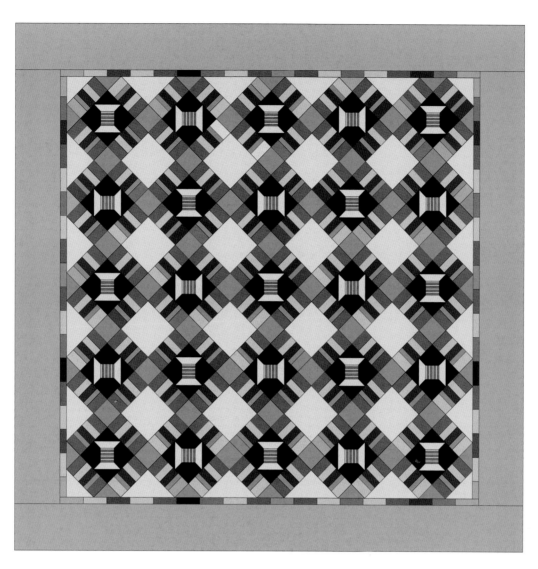

Spools *approximate size 73" x 73"*

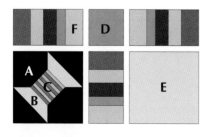

*Alternate
Easy Empty Spool
block*

Fabric Requirements: *color photo on page 35 & 53*

Fabric A *(Dark print)*	$1^{1}/8$ yard
Fabric B *(Assorted medium prints)*	$^{5}/8$
Fabric C *(Stripes)***	$^{1}/4$
Fabric D *(Medium print)*	$2^{7}/8$*
Fabric E *(Light print)*	1

Fabric F *(Assorted medium prints that are not as dark as A and not as light as E)*

fat quarters	**25 OR**
scraps to equal	(50) 4" x 20" rectangles

* includes binding
**for threaded spools only

Cutting Instructions for Spools

Fabric A
3 strips $3^5/8$" wide   Cut into (25) $3^5/8$" squares
5 strips $3^1/4$" wide   Cut into (50) $3^1/4$" squares

Fabric B
3 strips $3^5/8$" wide   Cut into (25) $3^5/8$" squares – *in matching sets of 2*

**Fabric C
2 strips $2^1/2$" wide   Cut into (25) $2^1/2$" squares

Fabric D
1 strip $5^1/2$" wide   Cut into (6) $5^1/2$" squares cut in half diagonally twice
4 strips $3^1/2$" wide   Cut into (40) $3^1/2$" squares

Outer Border
8 strips $5^1/2$" wide

Binding
8 strips $2^1/2$" wide

Fabric E
3 strips   6" wide   Cut into (16) 6" squares
                                    (2) $4^7/8$" squares cut in half diagonally once *(corner triangles)*
1 strip $9^1/4$" wide   Cut into (4) $9^1/4$" squares cut in half diagonally twice

---

Fabric F
cut along the 20" width of fat quarters
50 strips   4" x 20" wide   From each strip cut (2) each of the following pieces:
                                          $1^1/4$" x 4"
                                          $1^1/2$" x 4"
                                          $1^3/4$" x 4"
                                          2" x 4"
                                          $2^1/4$" x 4"

Pieced Accent Border
Fabric F scraps   (72) $1^1/2$" x 4" rectangles

**If making spools with set in seams gives you the shivers, do not cut these pieces. Instead cut:
Fabric B
3 strips $1^7/8$" wide   Cut into (50) $1^7/8$" squares – *in matching sets of 2*
and make the spools as instructed in Easy Empty Spools.

Sewing Instructions

Spools of Thread

Place fabric A and B 3⁵/₈" squares right sides together making sure all edges are even. Cut them in half diagonally. Sew triangles together on the wide edge. Press seam towards darker fabric and trim off dog ears. Handle bias edges carefully while sewing and pressing.

Figure 1

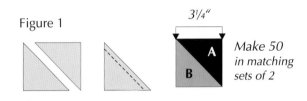

3¹/₄"

Make 50 in matching sets of 2

3⁵/₈" squares fabrics A and B

Measure 1¹/₄" from the seam of the half square triangles and **_trim corner of fabric B section_** as illustrated in Figure 2.

Figure 2

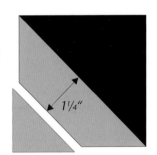

1¹/₄"

Measure 1¹/₄" from the diagonal center of fabric A 3¹/₄" square *(marked by the dotted line)* and trim corner as before. Refer to Figure 3.

Figure 3

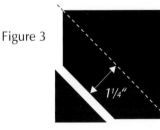

Trim corner from 50 fabric A 3¹/₄" squares

1¹/₄"

On the wrong side of fabric C 2¹/₂" squares, mark each corner ¹/₄" from the edge as illustrated in Figure 4.

Figure 4

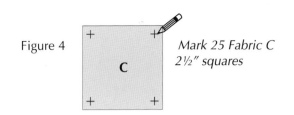

Mark 25 Fabric C 2½" squares

C

With right sides together, place fabric C 2¹/₂" square on top of a trimmed half square triangle as illustrated in Figure 5. Sew in-between the marks. Backstitch a few stitches at the beginning and end of the seam.

NOTE: *If you are using striped fabric for the thread, be sure the stripes are going in the proper direction.*

Start and end stitching exactly at the hatch marks

Figure 5

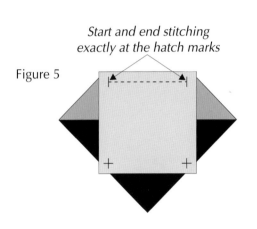

Repeating these steps, apply another trimmed half square triangle to opposite side of the Fabric C 2¹/₂" square.

Following the same steps, apply the trimmed fabric A pieces to the remaining free sides of the fabric C 2¹/₂" square. Remember to backstitch these seams.

Fold spool unit in half so sides are even. Stitch seam starting at the outer edge sewing towards the seam intersection, backstitching a few stitches. Refer to Figure 6.

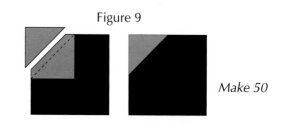

Figure 9

Make 50

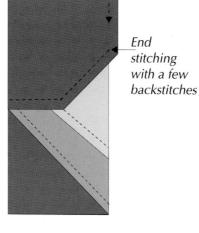

Figure 6

End stitching with a few backstitches

Repeat these steps on the remaining 3 seams.

Sew these units and half square triangles together as illustrated in Figure 10. Press seam as arrow indicates.

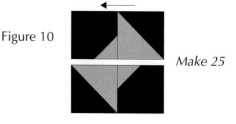

Figure 10

Make 25

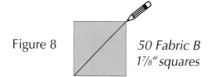

Figure 7

Make 25

Carefully press spool block.

EASY Empty Spools

(Use these instructions ONLY if you are not making spools with set in seams).

Follow the directions in "Spools of Thread" and make 50 fabric A/B half square triangles.

Draw a diagonal line on the wrong side of all fabric B 1⅞" squares *(see shortcuts)*.

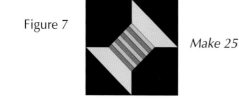

Figure 8

50 Fabric B 1⅞" squares

With right sides together, position a fabric B 1⅞" square on the corner of a fabric A 3¼" square. Stitch on the pencil line. Cut seam allowance to ¼" and press seam towards outer edge.

Pieced Sashing

Using only 1 piece from each size, sew fabric F pieces (1¼" – 1½" – 1¾" – 2" – 2¼") together into a strip set. Vary the order in each strip set. Press seam allowances in one direction. Make 100 strip sets.

Using a rotary cutter and ruler, trim strip set to measure 3½" as illustrated in Figure 11.

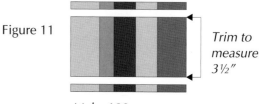

Figure 11

Trim to measure 3½"

Make 100

Then trim sides to measure 6" as illustrated in Figure 12.

Trim to measure 6"

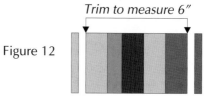

Figure 12

Refer to Figure 13 and arrange fabrics D and E squares/triangles with the units you have made. Sew pieces together to form rows. Press seams in block rows towards spools and fabric E squares/triangles. Press seams in sashing rows towards the cornerstones. Sew rows together and carefully press.

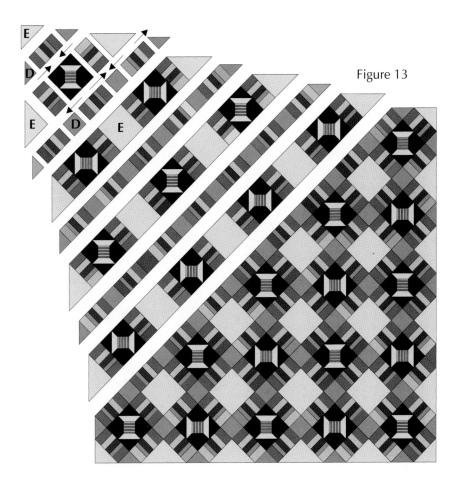

Figure 13

If necessary trim setting triangles so quilt edge is even.

Pieced Accent Border
For each side, sew (18) 1^1/$_2$" x 4" fabric F pieces together lengthwise. Make 4.

Measure the length of your quilt *(through the middle of the quilt)* and trim 2 pieced accent border units to that measurement. Sew to each side of the quilt and press seams towards quilt. Apply accent border to top and bottom of the quilt using the same technique.

Outer Border
Measure the length of your quilt again and piece 2 fabric D border strips (5^1/$_2$") to that length. Sew to each side of the quilt. Press seams towards outer edge. Repeat these steps for the top and bottom.

In Search of Hemingway *approximate size 87" x 101"*

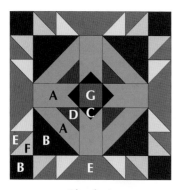

Block A

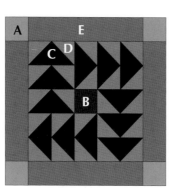

Block B

Fabric Requirements: *color photo on page 38 & 47*

Fabric A *(Assorted animal prints)* 2¹/₄ yards
Fabric B *(Black/green print)* 3³/₄*
Fabric C *(Black)* 2
Fabric D *(Burgundy)* 2⁵/₈
Fabric E *(Olive)* 3¹/₂
Fabric F *(Assorted Golds)* 1¹/₄

*includes binding

Cutting Instructions for In Search of Hemingway & Country Manor

Fabric A *(If you are using assorted prints, **cut squares and rectangles in matching sets of 4**)*
◣ 3 strip 2⁷/₈" wide Cut into (30) 2⁷/₈" squares
◣ 4 strip 4⁷/₈" wide Cut into (30) 4⁷/₈" squares
  4 strip 4¹/₂" wide Cut into (60) 4¹/₂" x 2¹/₂" rectangles
  6 strip 2¹/₂" wide Cut into (84) 2¹/₂" squares

Fabric B
◣ 4 strips 4⁷/₈" wide Cut into (30) 4⁷/₈" squares
  7 strips 2¹/₂" wide Cut into (99) 2¹/₂" squares

Border
9 strips 6¹/₂" wide

Binding
10 strips 2¹/₂" wide

Fabric C
◣ 3 strips 2⁷/₈" wide Cut into (30) 2⁷/₈" squares
  12 strips 4¹/₂" wide Cut into (180) 4¹/₂" x 2¹/₂" rectangles

---

Fabric D
27 strips 2¹/₂" wide Cut into (420) 2¹/₂" squares

Accent Border
9 strips 1¹/₂" wide

Fabric E
◣ 5 strips 2⁷/₈" wide Cut into (60) 2⁷/₈" squares
  28 strips 2¹/₂" wide Cut into (82) 2¹/₂" x 10¹/₂" rectangles
         from the leftovers Cut (28) 2¹/₂" x 6¹/₂" rectangles
  2 strips 6¹/₂" wide Cut into (32) 2¹/₂" x 6¹/₂" rectangles

Fabric F
◣ 5 strips 2⁷/₈" wide Cut into (60) 2⁷/₈" squares
  8 strips 2¹/₂" wide Cut into (120) 2¹/₂" squares

Fabric G
1 strip 2¹/₂" wide Cut into (15) 2¹/₂" squares

◣ Do NOT cut these strips if you plan on making half square triangles by drawing a grid or using products such as Triangle Paper™

Fabric Requirements for Country Manor

color photo on page 41 & 48

Light	1¹/4 yards
Medium lights *(Tans)*	³/8 yard of 15 fabrics
Medium darks	¹/4 yard of 15 fabrics
Darks	¹/4 yard of 24 fabrics
Accent border	¹/2 yard
Outer border/Binding	2⁵/8 yard

Fabric Substitution Guide for Country Manor

(Use cutting instructions on page 93)

Fabric A	*Tans*
Fabric B	*Darks*
Fabric C	*Darks*
Fabric D	*Medium darks - Block A*
	Tans - Block B
Fabric E	*Medium darks*
Fabric F	*Light*
Fabric G	*Darks*

Sewing Instructions

Block A

Use your favorite technique to make half square triangles *(see shortcuts)* or use the following method.

Place fabric squares right sides together. Cut them in half diagonally. Sew triangles together on the wide edge. Press towards darker fabric and trim off dog ears. Handle bias edges carefully when sewing and pressing.

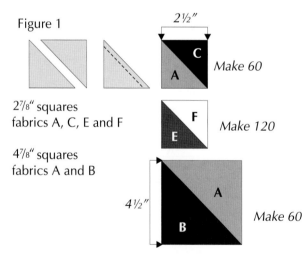

Figure 1

2⁷/8" squares
fabrics A, C, E and F

4⁷/8" squares
fabrics A and B

C
A
Make 60

F
E
Make 120

4¹/2"
A
B
Make 60

Using a sharp pencil, draw a diagonal line on the wrong side of fabric A/C 2¹/2" half square triangles. Refer to Figure 2.

Figure 2

*60 fabric A/C
2¹/2" half square triangles*

Place the half square triangles onto a corresponding fabric A 2¹/2" x 4¹/2" rectangle as illustrated in Figure 3. Sew on the pencil line. Trim seam allowance to ¹/4" and press as arrows indicate.

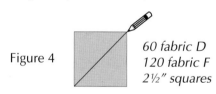

Figure 3

A
Make 60

Draw a diagonal line on the wrong side of fabric D and F 2¹/2" squares *(see shortcuts)*.

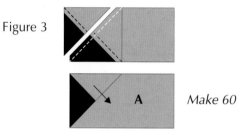

Figure 4

*60 fabric D
120 fabric F
2¹/2" squares*

Place a fabric D 2¹/2" square on the corner of the fabric A section of the A/B 4¹/2" half square triangle. Stitch on the pencil line. Refer to Figure 5. Cut seam allowance to ¹/4" and press towards outer edge.

Figure 5

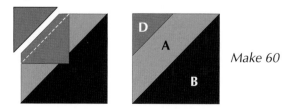

D
A
B
Make 60

Arrange fabric G 2^1/2" square and units you've made as illustrated in Figure 6. Sew together to form 3 horizontal rows. Press seams as arrows indicate. Sew rows together.

Figure 6

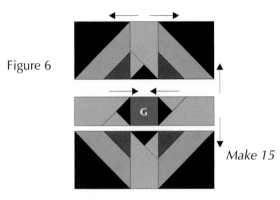

Make 15

Sew a fabric B 2^1/2" square onto 60 fabric E/F half square triangles as illustrated in Figure 7.

Figure 7

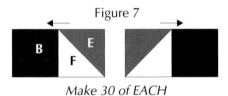

Make 30 of EACH

With right sides together, position a fabric F 2^1/2" square on the corner of a fabric E 2^1/2" x 6^1/2" rectangle. Stitch on the pencil line. Cut seam allowance to ^{1}/4" and press. Repeat these steps for the other side.

Figure 8

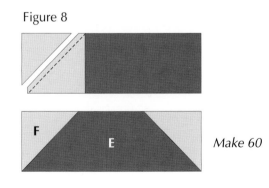

Make 60

Sew remaining half square triangles and the units you've made together as illustrated in Figure 9.

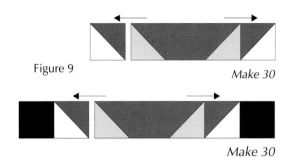

Figure 9

Make 30

Make 30

Sew these units onto the block as illustrated in Figure 10. Press seams as arrows indicate.

Figure 10

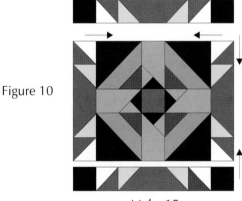

Make 15

Block B

Draw a diagonal line on 360 fabric D 2^1/2" squares *(see shortcuts)*.

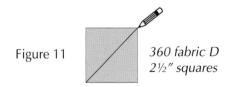

Figure 11

360 fabric D 2½" squares

With right sides together, position a fabric D 2^1/2" square on the corner of a fabric C 2^1/2" x 4^1/2" rectangle. Stitch on the pencil line.

Cut seam allowance to ^{1}/4" and press towards outer edge. Repeat steps for the other corner.

Figure 12

Make 180

Sew 3 units together as illustrated in Figure 13. Press seams in the direction of arrow.

Figure 13

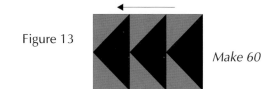

Make 60

With right sides together, sew ²/₃ of a fabric B 2¹/₂" square onto the unit as illustrated in Figure 14. Fingerpress this partial seam as arrow indicates.

Figure 14

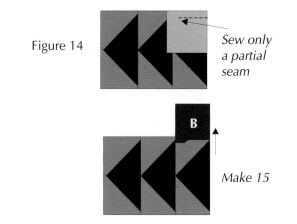

Sew only a partial seam

Make 15

Add the next 3 sections in the order illustrated in Figure 15. Carefully press each seam as you go along. The last seam will complete the partial seam you started with.

Figure 15

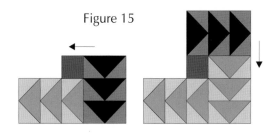

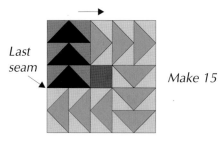

Last seam

Make 15

Sew fabric A and B 2¹/₂" squares onto each end of fabric E 2¹/₂" x 10¹/₂" rectangles. Refer to Figure 16. Press seams as arrows indicate.

Figure 16

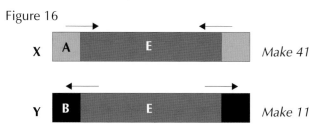

Make 41

Make 11

Sew remaining fabric E 2¹/₂" x 10¹/₂" rectangles onto each side of Block B as illustrated in Figure 17. Press seams as arrows indicate.

Figure 17

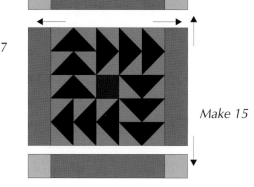

Make 15

Sew the pieced sections X onto the top and bottom of each block.

Putting the Quilt Together

Arrange Blocks A and B as illustrated in Figure 18. Sew blocks together to form horizontal rows and then sew the rows together.

Figure 18

NOTE: Keep Block A and B orientation consistently matching Figures 10 & 17 to insure easy seam butting.

Sew remaining sections X and Y together as illustrated in Figure 18, ***paying special attention to their color sequence.***

Sew these pieced sections to each side of the quilt. Press seams towards outer edge. Sew sections to the top and bottom of the quilt adding fabric A or B 2$^{1}/_{2}$" squares onto ends as appropriate.

Border

Measure the length of your quilt *(through the middle of the quilt)* and piece fabric D border strips (1$^{1}/_{2}$") to that length. Sew to each side of the quilt and press seams towards outer edge.

Using the same techniques, apply border strips to the top and bottom of your quilt.

Repeat these steps, this time using fabric B (6$^{1}/_{2}$") strips.

Days of Wine & Roses *approximate size 84" x 102"*

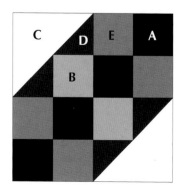

Fabric Requirements: *color photo on page 12 & 61*

Fabric A *(Burgundy)*	5* yards
Fabric B *(Rose)*	2$\frac{1}{3}$
Fabric C *(Peach)*	1$\frac{1}{8}$
Fabric D *(Charcoal)*	$\frac{7}{8}$
Fabric E *(Red)*	2$\frac{1}{4}$
Fabric F *(Sashing)*	
Border Stripes *cut lengthwise*	2$\frac{3}{4}$
(5 Border Stripes at least 3$\frac{1}{2}$" wide) **OR**	
Yardage *cut across width*	1$\frac{1}{3}$

*includes binding

Cutting Instructions for Days of Wine & Roses

Fabric A

11 strips	$7^{1}/_{4}$" wide	Cut into (52) $7^{1}/_{4}$" squares cut in half diagonally twice
3 strips	$5^{1}/_{8}$" wide	Cut into (17) $5^{1}/_{8}$" squares
1 strip	$3^{7}/_{8}$" wide	Cut into (10) $3^{7}/_{8}$" squares cut in half diagonally once *(corner triangles)*
1 strip	$3^{1}/_{2}$" wide	Cut into (8) $3^{1}/_{2}$" x ** *(make this part of the measurement match the width of YOUR sashing strips)*
12 strips	$2^{5}/_{8}$" wide	

Binding

10 strips	$2^{1}/_{2}$" wide	

Fabric B

2 strips	$5^{1}/_{8}$" wide	Cut into (10) $5^{1}/_{8}$" squares
9 strips	$4^{3}/_{4}$" wide	Cut into (70) $4^{3}/_{4}$" squares
6 strips	$2^{5}/_{8}$" wide	Cut into (80) $2^{5}/_{8}$" squares

Fabric C

6 strips	$5^{1}/_{8}$" wide	Cut into (40) $5^{1}/_{8}$" squares cut in half diagonally once

Fabric D

7 strips	3" wide	Cut into (80) 3" squares cut in half diagonally once

Fabric E

2 strips	$7^{1}/_{4}$" wide	Cut into (8) $7^{1}/_{4}$" squares cut in half diagonally twice
4 strips	$5^{1}/_{8}$" wide	Cut into (27) $5^{1}/_{8}$" squares
12 strips	$2^{5}/_{8}$" wide	

Fabric F *(You can use either border stripes or an all over print)*
  Option 1: *Fabric cut the length of the fabric*
4 border strips   cut into $2^{3}/_{4}$ yard lengths

  Option 2: *Fabric cut across the width and pieced*
10 strips $3^{3}/_{4}$"* wide   *or any width you choose*
NOTE: You will need to add yardage if you use wider sashing strips.

Sewing Instructions

Section 1

Sew fabric A and E $2^{5}/_{8}$" strips together lengthwise as indicated in Figure 1. Press seam towards darker fabric. Cutting across pieced strip, cut into $2^{5}/_{8}$" sections.

Figure 1

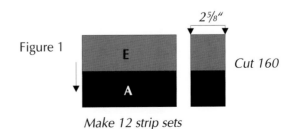

Make 12 strip sets

Make a 4-patch checkerboard by sewing 2 sections together. Press as arrow indicates.

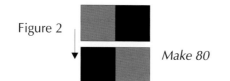

Figure 2

Make 80

Section 2

Sew 2 fabric D triangles onto fabric B 2⅝" square as illustrated in Figure 3. Press seams as arrows indicate, being careful not to stretch the bias edges of the triangles.

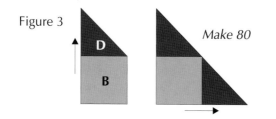

Figure 3

D

B

Make 80

Sew a fabric C triangle onto this unit as illustrated in Figure 4. Press seam as arrow indicates.

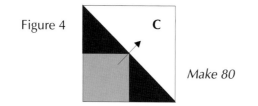

Figure 4

C

Make 80

Sew sections 1 and 2 together to form block. Press seam as arrows indicate. Refer to Figure 5.

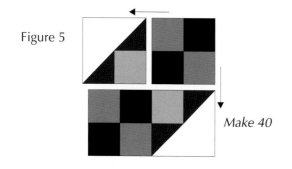

Figure 5

Make 40

Section 3

Sew 2 fabric A triangles onto fabric B 4¾" square. Press seams as arrows indicate.

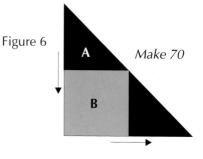

Figure 6

A

B

Make 70

Sew sections 3 onto blocks as illustrated in Figure 7. Press seams as arrows indicate. Handle bias edges carefully.

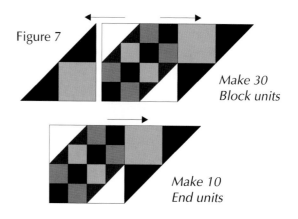

Figure 7

Make 30 Block units

Make 10 End units

Sew 6 block units together to make a row. Refer to Figure 8. Make 5 rows.

Figure 8

Make 5 rows

Half Square Triangles

Place 5⅛" squares right sides together. Cut them in half diagonally. Sew triangles together on the wide edge. Press seam towards darker fabric and trim off dog ears. Refer to Figure 9.

Figure 9

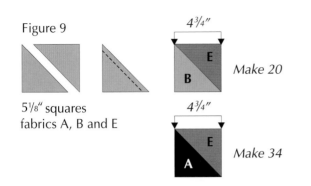

5⅛" squares
fabrics A, B and E

Make 20

Make 34

Sew fabric A triangles onto B/E half square triangle as illustrated in Figure 10. Press seams as arrows indicate.

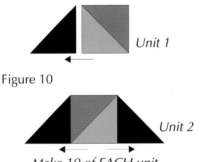

Unit 1

Figure 10

Unit 2

Make 10 of EACH unit

Sew these units to block end units as illustrated in Figure 11. Press seams as arrows indicate. Sew these pieced block units to the ends of each row.

Figure 11

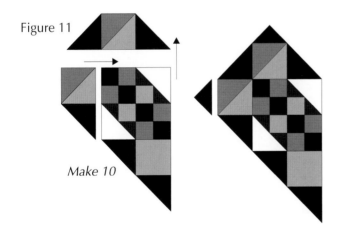

Make 10

Refer to Figure 16 for a quilt overview and apply fabric A triangles to all 4 corners of row sections except those that will be getting the border corner units.

Sashing

Measure the length of the row sections, subtract 6" from that number. Make 4 fabric F sashing strips to that length. Piece these strips if necessary.

❤

IMPORTANT NOTE: *If your rows have a slight size variation, use the average measurement and cut all sashing strips to that one length.*

Sew fabric A 3½" x *(width of sashing strip)* rectangle onto each end of the sashing strips. Press seam towards sashing.

Sew one sashing strip to each row. Press seam towards sashing. Using a ruler and a sharp pencil, mark block match points on the sashing strip as illustrated in Figure 12. Sew quilt rows together matching block points to marks and press.

Figure 12

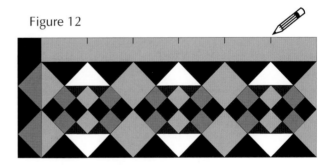

Pieced Border

Sew a fabric A and E triangle onto the A/E half square triangle as illustrated in Figure 13.

Figure 13

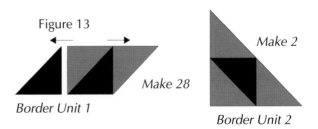

Make 2

Make 28

Border Unit 1

Border Unit 2

Sew **14** Border Units 1 together. Add 1 Border Unit 2 as illustrated in Figure 14.

Figure 14

Make 2

Sew pieced borders to sides of quilt and press seam towards outer edge. Refer to Figure 16.

Corners

Sew a fabric A triangle onto each side of A/E half square triangle, paying attention to the orientation of the half square triangle. Add small fabric A triangle to corner. Refer to Figure 15.

Figure 15

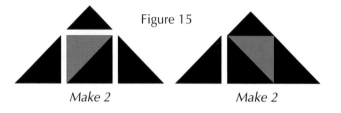

Make 2   *Make 2*

Sew corner sections onto quilt. Press seams towards outer edge.

Figure 16

Baker Street *approximate size 84" x 102"*

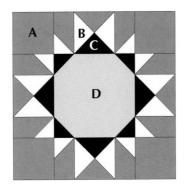

Fabric Requirements: *color photo on page 23 & 58*

Fabric A *(Tan)*	6³/8* yards
Fabric B *(White)*	3
Fabric C *(Black)*	2¹/3
Fabric D *(Beige print)*	1¹/4

*includes binding

Cutting Instructions for Baker Street

Fabric A

4 strips	4^1/$_4$" wide	Cut into (32) 4^1/$_4$" squares
22 strips	3^1/$_2$" wide	Cut into (256) 3^1/$_2$" x 2" rectangles *and* (80) 3^1/$_2$" squares
7 strips	6^1/$_2$" wide	Cut into (17) 6^1/$_2$" squares *and* (14) 6^1/$_2$" x 9^1/$_2$" rectangles

Border

4 strips	2^5/$_8$" wide	Cut into (50) 2^5/$_8$" squares *and* (2) 2^5/$_8$" x 4^3/$_4$" rectangles
9 strips	3^1/$_2$" wide	

Binding

10 strips	2^1/$_2$" wide	

Fabric B

8 strips	4^1/$_4$" wide	Cut into (64) 4^1/$_4$" squares
13 strips	2" wide	Cut into (256) 2" squares

Border

7 strips	4^1/$_4$" wide	Cut into (52) 4^1/$_4$" squares cut in half diagonally twice
	scraps	Cut into (2) 4" squares cut in half diagonally once *(corner triangles)*

Fabric C

4 strips	4^1/$_4$" wide	Cut into (32) 4^1/$_4$" squares
7 strips	2" wide	Cut into (128) 2" squares

Border

4 strips	2^5/$_8$" wide	Cut into (50) 2^5/$_8$" squares *and* (2) 2^5/$_8$" x 4^3/$_4$" rectangles
16 strips	2" wide	

Fabric D

6 strips	6^1/$_2$" wide	Cut into (32) 6^1/$_2$" squares

Sewing Instructions

Section 1

Layer fabric A and B 4¹/₄" squares right sides together, making sure all edges are even. Press fabrics together. On the wrong side of the lighter fabric, draw a line across the square diagonally *(see shortcuts)*. Sew ¹/₄" on each side of this line. Carefully cut the square in half as illustrated in Figure 1.

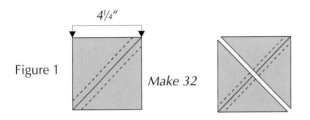

Figure 1

4¹/₄"

Make 32

Cut triangles in half again, this time on the pencil line. Press seam towards darker fabric. Handle triangles carefully to not stretch bias edges.

Repeat these steps, this time using fabric B and C.

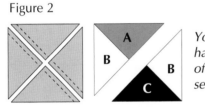

Figure 2

You will have 128 of each set

A

B

B

C

Sew pieced triangles together as illustrated in Figure 3 paying special attention to the color layout. Press this seam open.

Figure 3

Make 128

♥

NOTE: *To achieve a nicely joined seam intersection, nestle intersecting seams together before sewing. Do NOT place a pin at the intersecting point.*

Section 2

Draw a diagonal line on the wrong side of all 2" fabric B squares *(see shortcuts)*.

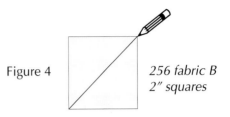

Figure 4

256 fabric B 2" squares

With right sides together, position a fabric B 2" square on the corner of a fabric A 2" x 3¹/₂" rectangle. Stitch on the pencil line.

Cut seam allowance to ¹/₄" and press seams as arrows indicate. Refer to Figure 5. Make sure you are stitching at the correct angles.

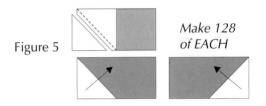

Figure 5

Make 128 of EACH

Sew sections 1 and 2 together as illustrated in Figure 6.

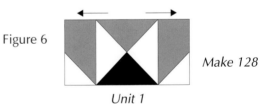

Figure 6

Make 128

Unit 1

Section 3

Draw a diagonal line on the wrong side of all 2" fabric C squares.

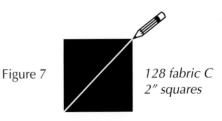

Figure 7

128 fabric C 2" squares

With right sides together, sew a fabric C 2" square on each corner of a fabric D 6¹/₂" square. Cut seam allowance to ¹/₄" and press towards outer edge.

Figure 8

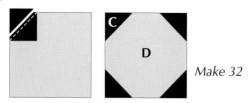

Make 32

Sew Unit 1 onto each side of section 3 as illustrated in Figure 9. Press seams as arrows indicate.

Figure 9

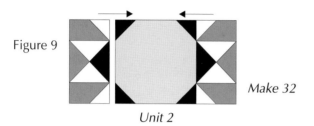

Make 32

Unit 2

Sew a fabric A 3¹/2" square onto each end of the remaining Units 1 as illustrated in Figure 10. Press seam as arrow indicates.

Figure 10

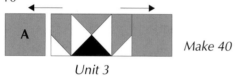

Make 40

Unit 3

Sew units together as illustrated in Figure 11.

Figure 11

*Block A
Make 20*

Sew Units 1 and fabric A 6¹/2" square together as illustrated in Figure 12. Pay special attention to the orientation of Units 1.

Figure 12

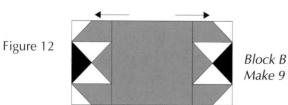

*Block B
Make 9*

Sew Unit 1 and fabric A 9¹/2" x 6¹/2" rectangle together as illustrated in Figure 13.

Figure 13

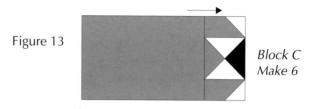

*Block C
Make 6*

Arrange blocks A, B, C along with remaining Units 2, fabric A 6¹/2" squares and 6¹/2" x 9¹/2" rectangles as illustrated in Figure 14. Sew together to form horizontal rows.

Figure 14

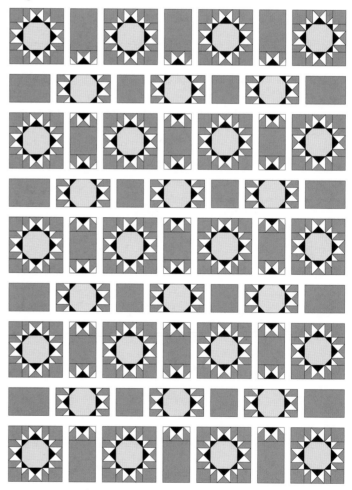

Sew rows together and carefully press quilt.

BORDER

Measure the length of your quilt *(through the middle of the quilt)* and piece 2 fabric C 2" strips to that measurement. Sew to each side of quilt and press seam towards outer edge.

Using the same technique, apply fabric C strips to the top and bottom of your quilt.

Pieced Border

Sew fabric B triangles onto fabric A and C $2^5/8$" squares as illustrated in Figure 15. Press seams towards darker fabric.

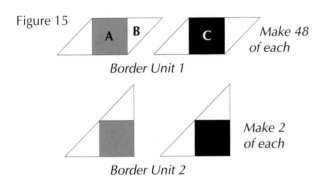

Figure 15

A B

C

Make 48 of each

Border Unit 1

Make 2 of each

Border Unit 2

Border Sides: *Make 2*

Sew **27** fabric A and C Border Units 1 together alternating colors. Add 1 Border Unit 2. Refer to Figure 16.

Figure 16

Border Top and Bottom: *Make 2*

Sew **21** fabric A and C Border Units 1 together. Add 1 Border Unit 2.

Sew pieced borders to sides of quilt and press seams towards quilt. Then sew pieced border to the top and bottom of quilt.

Border Corners

Add a fabric B triangle onto each side of fabric A and C $2^5/8$" x $4^3/4$" rectangle and press. Add fabric B corner triangles as indicated in Figure 17.

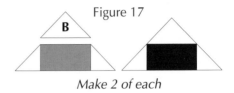

Figure 17

B

Make 2 of each

Sew corner sections onto border as indicated in Figure 18.

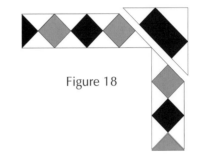

Figure 18

As before, apply fabric C 2" strips to the quilt. Press towards outer edge.

Apply fabric A $3^1/2$" outer border and press towards outer edge.

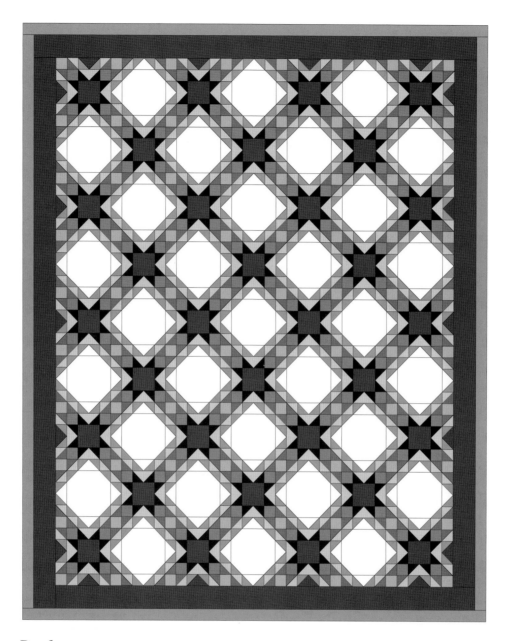

Daydreams *approximate size 88" x 108"*

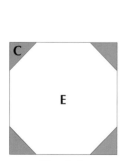

Block B

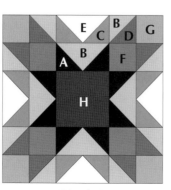

Block A

Fabric Requirements: *color photo on page 28 & 51*

Fabric A *(Dark Purple)*	$1^{1}/_{3}$ yards
Fabric B *(Gold)*	$2^{1}/_{4}$
Fabric C *(Green)*	$3^{3}/_{4}$*
Fabric D *(Purple print)*	$1^{1}/_{4}$
Fabric E *(Beige print)*	$3^{1}/_{4}$
Fabric F *(Medium Rust)*	$3/_{4}$
Fabric G *(Light Rust)*	$5/_{8}$
Fabric H *(Rust Print)*	$2^{1}/_{2}$

includes binding

Cutting Instructions for Daydreams

Fabric A		
16 strips	$2^1/2$" wide	Cut into (256) $2^1/2$" squares
Fabric B		
8 strips	$4^1/2$" wide	Cut into (128) $2^1/2$" x $4^1/2$"
◣ 12 strips	$2^7/8$" wide	Cut into (142) $2^7/8$" squares
Fabric C		
26 strips	$2^1/2$" wide	Cut into (408) $2^1/2$" squares
Outer Border		
11 strips	$2^1/2$" wide	
Binding		
11 strips	$2^1/2$" wide	
Fabric D		
◣ 12 strips	$2^7/8$" wide	Cut into (142) $2^7/8$" squares
Fabric E		
8 strips	$8^1/2$" wide	Cut into (31) $8^1/2$" squares
8 strips	$4^1/2$" wide	Cut into (124) $2^1/2$" x $4^1/2$" rectangles
Fabric F		
8 strips	$2^1/2$" wide	Cut into (128) $2^1/2$" squares
Fabric G		
5 strips	$2^1/2$" wide	Cut into (80) $2^1/2$" squares
Fabric H		
5 strips	$4^1/2$" wide	Cut into (32) $4^1/2$" squares *and* (18) $2^1/2$" x $4^1/2$" rectangles
Inner Border		
10 strips	$5^1/2$" wide	

◣ Do NOT cut these strips if you plan on making half square triangles by drawing a grid or using products such as Triangle Paper™

Sewing Instructions

Block A

Draw a diagonal line on the wrong side of all fabric A and C 2½" squares (*see shortcuts*).

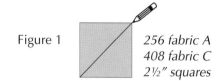

Figure 1

256 fabric A
408 fabric C
2½" squares

With right sides together, position a 2½" square on the corner of a 2½" x 4½" rectangle. Stitch on the pencil line. Cut seam allowance to ¼" and press seam towards outer edge. Repeat these steps for the other corner. Refer to Figure 2.

Figure 2

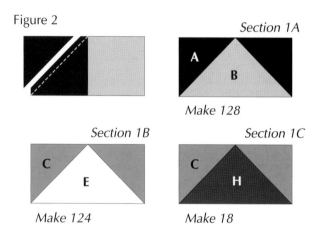

Section 1A

A
B

Make 128

Section 1B

C
E

Make 124

Section 1C

C
H

Make 18

Sew sections 1A to each side of fabric H 4½" square. Press seams as arrows indicate.

Figure 3

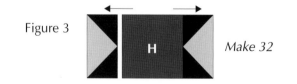

H

Make 32

Sew a fabric F 2½" square onto each end of remaining sections 1A. Press seams as arrows indicate.

Figure 4

F

Make 64

Sew these sections together as illustrated in Figure 5. Press seams as arrows indicate.

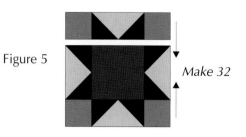

Figure 5

Make 32

Half Square Triangles

Use your favorite technique to make half square triangles (*see shortcuts*) or use the following method.

Place fabric B and D 2⅞" squares right sides together making sure all edges are even. Cut them in half diagonally. Sew triangles together on the wide edge. Press seam towards darker fabric and trim off dog ears. Handle bias edges carefully while sewing and pressing.

Figure 6

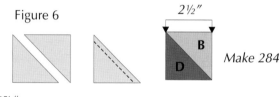

2½"

B
D

Make 284

2⅞" squares
fabrics B and D

Sew half square triangles, fabric G 2½" squares and sections 1B and 1C together as illustrated in Figure 7. Press seams as arrows indicate.

Figure 7

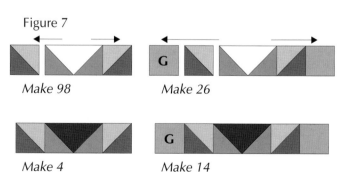

Make 98 *Make 26*

G

Make 4 *Make 14*

G

Block B

With right sides together, position a fabric C $2^{1}/2"$ square on the corner of a fabric E $8^{1}/2"$ square. Stitch on the pencil line. Cut seam allowance to $^{1}/4"$ and press seams towards outer edge. Repeat these steps for all corners. Refer to Figure 8.

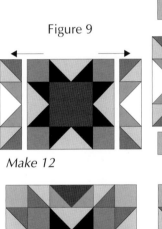

Figure 8

Make 31

Putting it All Together

Apply sections 2 to blocks A and B as illustrated in Figure 9. ***Pay attention to pressing arrows.***

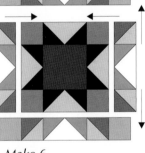

Figure 9

Make 12

Make 6

Make 10

Make 4

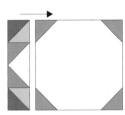

Make 8

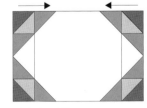

Make 15

Refer to Figure 10 and arrange blocks as illustrated. Sew blocks together to form rows. Press seams as arrows indicate. Then sew rows together.

Figure 10

Measure the length of your quilt *(through the middle of the quilt)* and piece 2 fabric H border strips ($5^{1}/2"$) to that length. Sew to each side of the quilt and press towards outer edge.

Apply border to top and bottom of the quilt using the same technique.

Repeat these steps for the outer border using fabric C strips ($2^{1}/2"$).

Times Remembered *approximate size 88" x 106"*

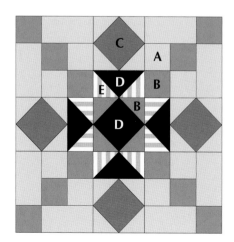

Fabric Requirements: *color photo on page 33 & 56*

Fabric A *(Cream/blue print)*	5^1/2 yards
Fabric B *(Medium blue 1)*	3
Fabric C *(Medium blue 2)*	3^1/8*
Fabric D *(Dark blue)*	2^3/4
Fabric E *(Blue/white stripe)*	1

includes binding

Cutting Instructions for Times Remembered

Fabric A

52 strips	2½" wide	Cut into (49) 2½" x 16½" rectangles
		use leftovers to cut some of the (320) 2½" squares
		leave 10 strips whole
10 strips	4½" wide	Cut into (80) 2½" x 4½" rectangles
		leave 5 strips whole

Fabric B

22 strips	2½" wide	Cut into (110) 2½" squares
		leave 15 strips whole
Border		
15 strips	2½" wide	Cut into (232) 2½" squares

Fabric C

10 strips	4½" wide	Cut into (80) 4½" squares
Outer Border		
10 strips	3" wide	
Binding		
10 strips	2½" wide	

Fabric D

8 strips	4½" wide	Cut into (20) 4½" squares *and*
		(80) 2½" x 4½" rectangles
Border		
11 strips	4½" wide	Cut into (58) 4½" squares *and*
		(58) 2½" x 4½" rectangles

Fabric E

10 strips	2½" wide	Cut into (160) 2½" squares

Sewing Instructions

Section 1

Sew fabric A (2½" and 4½") and fabric B (2½") strips together lengthwise as indicated in Figure 1. Press seam towards darker fabric. Cutting across the pieced strip, cut into 2½" sections.

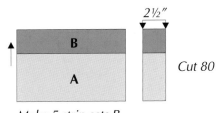

Make 5 strip sets B

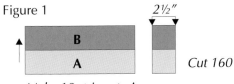

Figure 1

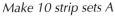

Make 10 strip sets A

Make a 4 patch checkerboard by sewing 2 strip sets A together. Refer to Figure 2. Add a fabric A 2½" x 4½" rectangle and then add strip set B section as illustrated. Press seams as arrows indicate.

113

Figure 2

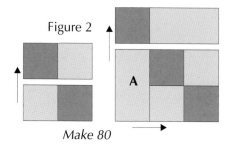

Make 80

Section 2

Draw a diagonal line on the wrong side of the indicated fabric A, B and E 2¹/2" squares *(see shortcuts).*

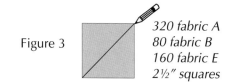

Figure 3

320 fabric A
80 fabric B
160 fabric E
2½" squares

With right sides together, position a fabric E 2¹/2" square on the corner of a fabric D 2¹/2" x 4¹/2" rectangle. Stitch on the pencil line. Press seams towards outer edge and then trim to ¹/4". Repeat these steps for the other corner. Refer to Figure 4.

Figure 4

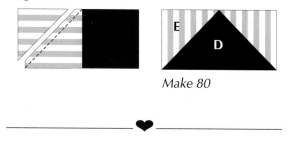

Make 80

♥

HINT: *If you are using stripes, place fabric E 2¹/2" squares as illustrated in Figure 4.*

Section 3

Starting at one corner, with right sides together, place a 2¹/2" square on top of a 4¹/2" square. Stitch on the pencil line. Press seams towards outer edge and then trim to ¹/4". Refer to Figure 5 for color designations.

Figure 5

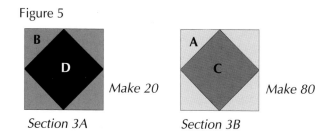

Make 20   *Make 80*

Section 3A   *Section 3B*

Sew sections 2 and 3B together as illustrated in Figure 6. Press seam as arrow indicates.

Figure 6

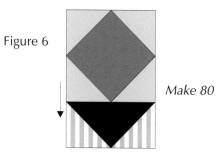

Make 80

Arrange sections as illustrated in Figure 7. Sew sections into 3 horizontal rows. Press seams as arrows indicate. Sew rows together to form block.

Figure 7

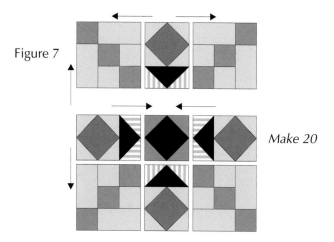

Make 20

On the wrong side of the 2¹/2" x 16¹/2" sashing strips, mark the center on each side as illustrated in Figure 8. Match these points to the center diamond tip of each block.

Figure 8

Mark center of sashing strips

Sew sashing strips in-between blocks as well as on the end of each row. Refer to Figure 9. Press seams towards sashing.

Figure 9

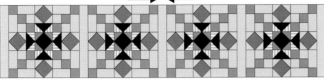

Make 5 rows

Sew fabric B 2½" squares and remaining fabric A sashing strips as illustrated in Figure 10. Press seams as arrows indicate.

Figure 10

Make 6

Sew pieced sashing strips to the top, bottom and in-between rows as illustrated in Figure 11.

Figure 11

Border

Using fabric D 4½" squares and fabric B 2½" squares, make 58 border squares. If necessary, refer to Section 3 for step-by-step instructions.

Figure 12

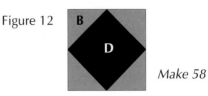

Make 58

Side Borders: *Make 2*

Starting and ending with a fabric D 2½" x 4½" rectangle, piece 16 rectangles and 15 border squares together. Refer to Figure 13.

Figure 13

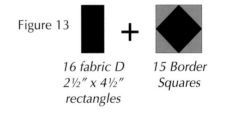

16 fabric D 2½" x 4½" rectangles   *15 Border Squares*

Top/Bottom Borders: *Make 2*

Starting and ending with a border square, piece 14 border squares and 13 fabric D rectangles together.

Figure 14

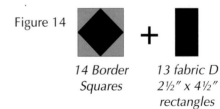

14 Border Squares   *13 fabric D 2½" x 4½" rectangles*

Sew pieced border to each side of your quilt. Press seams towards sashing. Sew pieced borders to the top and bottom of your quilt and press as before.

Outer Border

Measure the length of your quilt *(through the middle of the quilt)* and piece 2 fabric C outer border strips (3") to that measurement. Sew to each side of the quilt and press seams towards outer edge.

Using the same technique, apply the outer border to the top and bottom of your quilt.

Intrigue on the Orient Express *approximate size 87" x 104"*

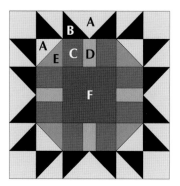

Fabric Requirements: *color photo on page 25 & 59*

Fabric A *(Peach)*	4⁷/₈ yards
Fabric B *(Dark Green/Black)*	1³/₄
Fabric C *(Medium Green)*	⁷/₈
Fabric D *(Purple)*	1¹/₄
Fabric E *(Orange/Rust)*	¹/₂
Fabric F *(Floral)*	4⁷/₈*

*includes binding

Cutting Instructions for Intrigue on the Orient Express

Fabric A

4 strips	12^1/$_2$" wide	Cut into (12) 12^1/$_2$" squares
5 strips	4^1/$_2$" wide	Cut into (80) 2^1/$_2$" x 4^1/$_2$" rectangles
5 strips	2^1/$_2$" wide	Cut into (80) 2^1/$_2$" squares
◣ 10 strips	2^7/$_8$" wide	Cut into (120) 2^7/$_8$" squares

Border

2 strips	8^1/$_2$" wide	Cut into (14) 4^1/$_2$" x 8^1/$_2$" rectangles
3 strips	4^1/$_2$" wide	Cut into (18) 4^1/$_2$" squares
3 strips	2^1/$_2$" wide	

Fabric B

10 strips	2^1/$_2$" wide	Cut into (160) 2^1/$_2$" squares
◣ 7 strips	2^7/$_8$" wide	Cut into (80) 2^7/$_8$" squares

Fabric C

10 strips	2" wide

Fabric D

5 strips	1^1/$_2$" wide

Border

3 strips	4^1/$_2$" wide	Cut into (18) 4^1/$_2$" squares
5 strips	2^1/$_2$" wide	

Fabric E

◣ 4 strips	2^7/$_8$" wide	Cut into (40) 2^7/$_8$" squares

Fabric F

3 strips	4^1/$_2$" wide	Cut into (20) 4^1/$_2$" squares

Border

3 strips	18^1/$_2$" wide*	Cut into (5) 18^1/$_2$" squares cut in half diagonally twice *(setting triangles)*
1 strip	9^1/$_2$" wide*	Cut into (2) 9^1/$_2$" squares cut in half diagonally once *(corner triangles)*
3 strips	8^1/$_2$" wide	Cut into (22) 8^1/$_2$" x 4^1/$_2$" rectangles
3 strips	4^1/$_2$" wide	Cut into (18) 4^1/$_2$" squares
3 strips	2^1/$_2$" wide	

Binding

10 strips	2^1/$_2$" wide

◣ Do NOT cut these strips if you plan on making half square triangles by drawing a grid or using products such as Triangle Paper™

If you like to use oversized setting and corner triangles cut these slightly larger.

Sewing Instructions

Section 1

Draw a diagonal line on the wrong side of 160 fabric B 2½" squares *(see shortcuts)*.

Figure 1   *160 Fabric B 2½" squares*

With right sides together, position a fabric B 2½" square on the corner of a fabric A 2½" x 4½" rectangle. Stitch on the pencil line. Cut seam allowance to ¼" and press towards outer edge. Repeat these steps for the other corner. Refer to Figure 2.

Figure 2

Make 80

Sew fabric C 2" strips and fabric D 1½" strip together lengthwise as illustrated in Figure 3. Cut into 2½" sections. Press seams as arrows indicate.

Figure 3   2½"

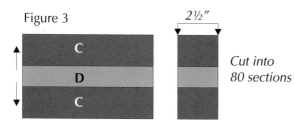

Cut into 80 sections

Make 5 strip sets

Sew the 2 units together as illustrated in Figure 4. Press seam as arrow indicates.

Figure 4

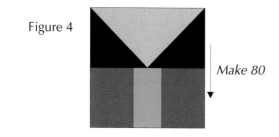

Make 80

Section 2

Use your favorite technique to make half square triangles *(see shortcuts)* or use the following method.

Place fabric A and E 2⅞" squares right sides together. Cut them in half diagonally. Sew triangles together on the wide edge to make the half square triangle. Press seam towards darker fabric and trim off dog ears.

Repeat these steps again only this time using fabric A and B 2⅞" squares. Refer to Figure 5.

Figure 5   2½"

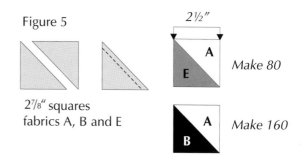

Make 80

Make 160

2⅞" squares fabrics A, B and E

Sew half square triangles together as illustrated in Figure 6, paying special attention to the orientation of the half square triangles. Press seam as arrow indicates.

Figure 6

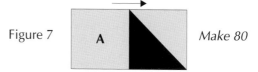

Make 80

Sew remaining fabric A/B half square triangles onto fabric A 2½" squares as illustrated in Figure 7.

Figure 7

Make 80

Sew these 2 units together as illustrated in Figure 8.

Figure 8

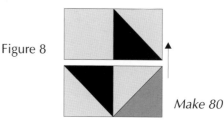

Make 80

Putting the Block Together

Arrange sections and fabric F 4½" square as illustrated in Figure 9. Sew pieces together to form 3 horizontal rows. Press seams as arrows indicate. Sew rows together to form block.

Figure 9

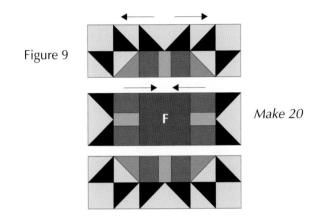

Make 20

BORDER

Refer to Figure 10 and sew the indicated 2½" fabric strips together lengthwise as illustrated. Cut into 2½" sections.

Figure 10

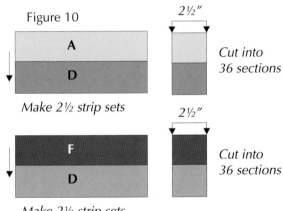

2½"

Cut into 36 sections

2½"

Cut into 36 sections

Make 2½ strip sets

Make 2½ strip sets

Sew sections together to make a 4-patch checkerboard as illustrated in Figure 11.

Figure 11

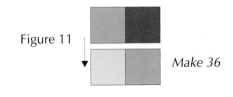

Make 36

Sew fabric A/F 4½" x 8½" rectangles and checkerboards together as illustrated in Figure 12.

Figure 12

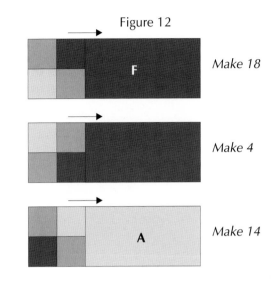

Make 18

Make 4

Make 14

Sew fabric A, D and F 4½" squares together as illustrated in Figure 13.

Figure 13

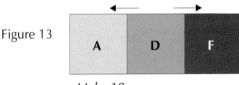

Make 18

Sew units together as illustrated in Figure 14. Press seams as arrows indicate.

Figure 14

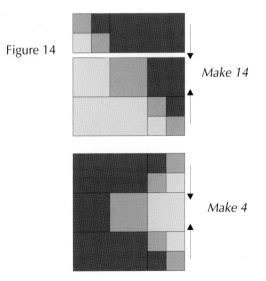

Make 14

Make 4

Sew blocks, fabric A 12½" squares, fabric F setting triangles and corner triangles together as diagramed in Figure 15. Make 2 of each row.

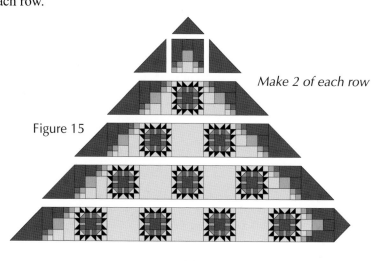

Make 2 of each row

Figure 15

---❤---

HINT: *Handle and press patchwork with care. Since blocks are set on point, the patchwork is vulnerable to being stretched out of shape until it is quilted.*

Sew rows together as illustrated in Figure 16. You will have 2 quilt halves. Sew quilt halves together. If necessary, trim setting triangles so quilt edge is even.

Figure 16

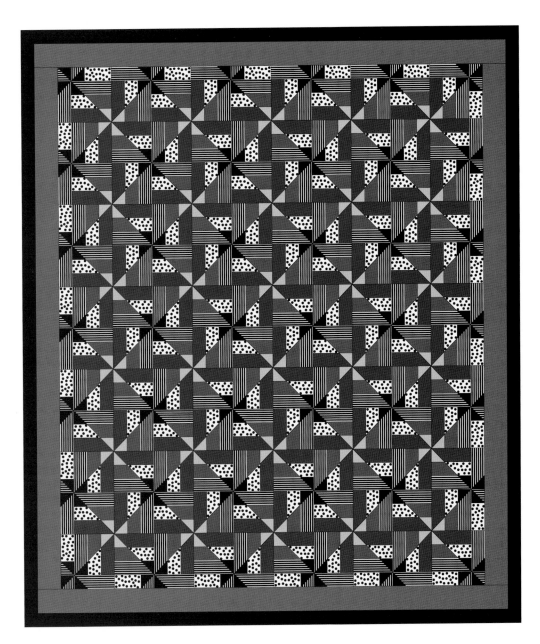

What A Wonderful Day! *approximate size 59" x 68"*

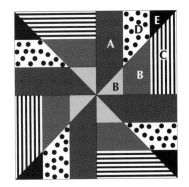

Fabric Requirements: *color photo on page 10 & 62*

Fabric A *(Assorted tone-on-tone dots)*	8 fat quarters
Fabric B *(Assorted wavy stripes)*	8 fat quarters
Fabric C *(Black/white stripes)*	1¹⁄₂ yards
Fabric D *(White with black dots)*	1
Fabric E *(Black)*	³⁄₄
Border #1 *(Print)*	⁷⁄₈
Border #2 *(Print)*	¹⁄₂
Binding *(Stripes)*	³⁄₄

Cutting Instructions for What a Wonderful Day!

Fabric A *(Assorted colors)*
Cut along the 18" edge of fat quarters

16 strips	5" wide	Cut into (120) 2" x 5" rectangles – *in sets of 4 of each color*

Fabric B *(Assorted colors)*
Cut along the 18" edge of fat quarters

16 strips	3½" wide	Cut into (120) 2" x 3½" rectangles – *in sets of 4 of each color*
16 strips	2" wide	Cut into (120) 2" squares – *in sets of 4 of each color*

Fabric C

8 strips	5" wide	Cut into (142) 2" x 5" rectangles
2 strips	2" wide	Cut into (26) 2" squares

Fabric D

8 strips	3½" wide	Cut into (142) 2" x 3½" rectangles

Fabric E

9 strips	2" wide	Cut into (168) 2" squares

Border #1

6 strips	4" wide

Border #2

6 strips	2" wide

Binding

7 strips	2½" wide

Sewing Instructions

Refer to Figure 1 and sew indicated 2" x 5" and 2" x 3½" rectangles and 2" squares together. Make sections A and B in matching color sets of 4. Press seams as arrows indicate.

Figure 1

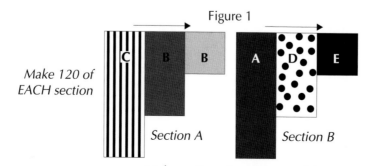

Make 120 of EACH section

Section A   Section B

Make sections in color sets of 4

Examine Figure 2. Using a rotary cutter and ruler carefully trim sections A and B as illustrated.

Figure 2

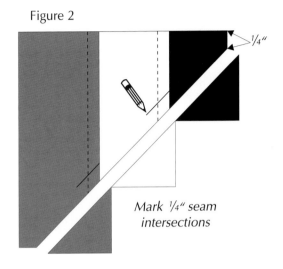

Mark ¼" seam intersections

Mark seam intersections on the wrong side of section B by drawing hatch marks ¼" from the cut edge as indicated in Figure 2.

Layer sections A and B right sides together. Using the hatch marks as seam matching points, pin intersecting seams together. Sew sections together and press as arrow indicates. Refer to Figure 3.

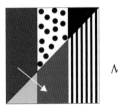

Figure 3

Make 120

Sew matching units together to make block as illustrated in Figure 4. Undo several stitches in the seam allowance of the pinwheel center and press seams in the direction the arrows indicate.

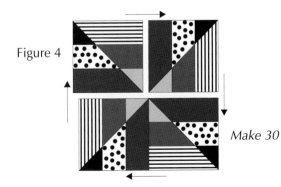

Figure 4

Make 30

HINT: Do not skip the pressing step illustrated in Figure 4 — you'll be very glad you used this technique when you are sewing the blocks together and all the seams butt easily.

Sew 5 blocks together to form a row. Press seams in one direction, alternating that direction with every row.

Figure 5

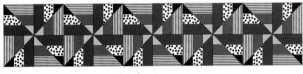

Make 6 rows

Sew rows together and press.

Inside Border

Using a sharp white pencil, draw a diagonal line on the wrong side of 48 fabric E 2" squares *(see shortcuts)*.

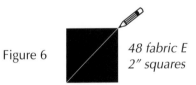

Figure 6   *48 fabric E 2" squares*

With right sides together position a fabric E 2" square on the corner of a fabric C 5" x 2" rectangle. Stitch on the pencil line. Cut seam allowance to ¼" and press towards outer edge.

Repeat these steps using fabric C and E 2" squares. Be sure stripes are pointing in the same direction as illustrated in Figure 7.

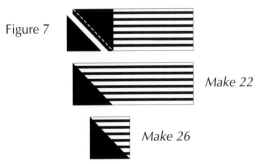

Figure 7

Make 22

Make 26

Figure 8

*Make 2 of
EACH*

Sew the inside border units you've made and fabric D 3¹/₂" x 2" rectangles together as illustrated in Figure 8. Make 2 of each border section.

Press seams in the opposite direction from the seams in the quilt top.

Starting with the side pieces, sew pieced inside border sections to quilt. Press seams towards the outer edge.

Repeat these steps and apply inside border sections to top and bottom of quilt.

Outer Borders

Measure the length of your quilt *(through the middle of the quilt)* and piece 2 border strips (4") to that length. Sew to each side of the quilt and press seams towards outer edge. Apply top and bottom using the same technique.

Repeat these steps for the second border using 2" strips.

Homemade Pie *approximate size 46" x 21"*

Fabric Requirements: *color photo on page 31 & 52*

Fabric A *(Apples)*	$^7/_8$ yard *(includes binding)*
Fabric B *(Cherries)*	$^1/_2$
Fabric C *(Burgundy)*	$^1/_3$
Fabric D *(Burgundy/white print)*	$^1/_2$

Cutting Instructions for Homemade Pie

Fabric A

1 strip	$6^1/_2$" wide	Cut into (3) $6^1/_2$" squares
3 strips	$2^1/_2$" wide	

Binding

4 strips	$2^1/_4$" wide

Fabric B

1 strip	14" wide	Cut into (1) 14" square cut in half diagonally twice *and* (2) $9^7/_8$" squares cut in half diagonally once *(corner triangles)*

Fabric C

5 strips	$1^1/_2$" wide

Fabric D

7 strips	$1^1/_2$" wide

Sewing Instructions

Sew fabric C and D 1½" fabric strips together length-wise as illustrated in Figure 1. Press seams towards darker fabric. Cutting across pieced strip sets, cut into 6½" and 1½" sections as indicated.

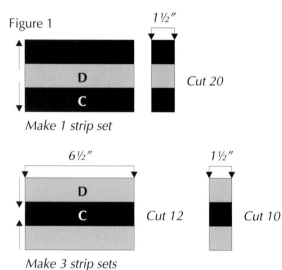

Figure 1

1½"

D

C

Cut 20

Make 1 strip set

6½"

1½"

D

C

Cut 12

Cut 10

Make 3 strip sets

Make a 9-patch checkerboard by sewing strip set sections together as illustrated in Figure 2. Press seams as arrows indicate.

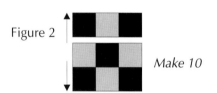

Figure 2

Make 10

Sew fabric A 6½" squares, fabric B triangles, strip set sections and checkerboards together as indicated in Figure 3.

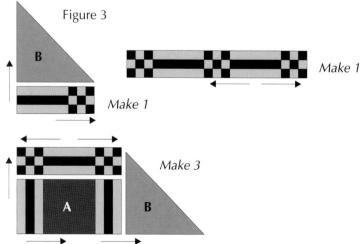

Figure 3

B

Make 1

Make 1

Make 3

A

B

Refer to Figure 4 and sew sections together in the order indicated. Press seams as arrows indicate.

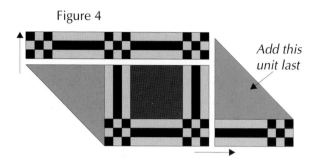

Figure 4

Add this unit last

Arrange corner triangles and the units you've made as illustrated in Figure 5 and sew together.

Figure 5

Border

If necessary, trim outer edge so it is even. Measure the length of your table runner *(through the middle)* and cut 2 fabric A 2½" strips to that measurement. Sew onto table runner and press seams towards outer edge. Repeat these steps to apply border to both ends of the table runner.

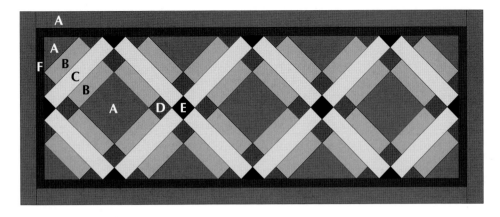

The Bounty of Harvest *approximate size 48" x 19"*

Fabric Requirements: *color photo on page 21 & 52*

Fabric A *(Floral)*	$^3/_4$ yard
Fabric B *(Stripes)*	$^1/_3$
Fabric C *(Gold print)*	$^1/_3$
Fabric D *(Dark green)*	$^1/_3$
Fabric E *(Rust)*	$^1/_8$
Fabric F *(Medium green)*	$^1/_2$ *(includes binding)*

Cutting Instructions for The Bounty of Harvest

Fabric A

1 strip	$6^1/_2$"	Cut into (3) $6^1/_2$" squares
1 strip	$9^3/_4$"	Cut into (1) $9^3/_4$" square cut in half diagonally twice *and* (2) $5^3/_8$" squares cut in half diagonally once *(corner triangles)*
4 strips	$1^3/_4$"	

Fabric B

4 strips	2" wide	Cut into (24) 2" x $6^1/_2$" rectangles

Fabric C

4 strips	2" wide	Cut into (12) 2" x $9^1/_2$" rectangles

Fabric D *(cut on the long edge of fat quarter)*

2 strips	2" wide	Cut into (16) 2" x 2" squares
1 strip	$3^1/_2$" wide	Cut into (4) $3^1/_2$" squares cut in half diagonally twice

Fabric E *(cut on the long edge of fat quarter)*

1 strip	$3^1/_2$" wide	Cut into (2) $3^1/_2$" squares cut in half diagonally twice *and* (2) 2" x 2" squares

continued

(Cutting Instructions for The Bounty of Harvest continued)

Fabric F

3 strips   1¼" wide

Binding

4 strips   2 ¼" wide

Sewing Instructions

Sew fabric D squares and triangles onto fabric B 2" x 6½" rectangles as indicated in Figure 1. Press seams as arrows indicate.

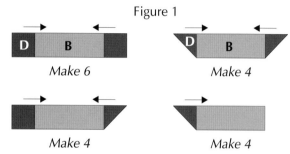

Figure 1

Make 6   *Make 4*

Make 4   *Make 4*

Sew 2 fabric B 2" x 6½" rectangles onto the sides of fabric A 6½" squares. Press seams as arrows indicate. Refer to Figure 2 and combine triangles and units as illustrated.

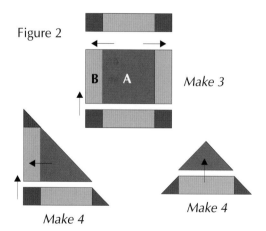

Figure 2

Make 3

Make 4   *Make 4*

Sew fabric E squares and triangles onto fabric C rectangles as indicated in Figure 3.

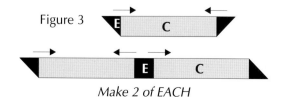

Figure 3

Make 2 of EACH

Sew remaining fabric C rectangles onto each side of checkerboard squares and press seams as arrows indicate.

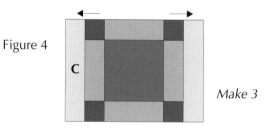

Figure 4

Make 3

Arrange units as illustrated in Figure 5 and sew together to form diagonal rows. Sew sashing in-between rows and press.

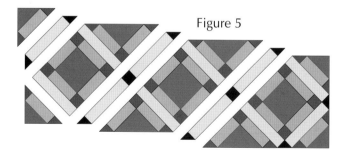

Figure 5

Border

If necessary, trim edges of table runner so they are even. Measure the length of the table runner *(through the middle)* and cut 2 fabric F 1¼" strips to that measurement. Sew onto table runner and press seams towards outer edge. Repeat these steps to apply fabric F strips to each end of the table runner.

Repeat these steps for the second border using fabric A 1¾" strips.

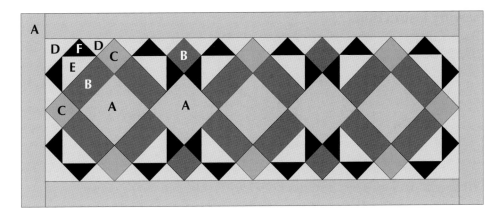

Celebrate the Seasons *approximate size 38" x 16"*

Fabric Requirements: *color photo on page 15 & 54*

Fabric A *(Floral)*	³/4 yard *(includes binding)*
Fabric B *(4 Purples)*	4 fat eighths
Fabric C *(Gold)*	1 fat eighth
Fabric D *(Light Yellow)*	1 fat quarter
Fabric E *(3 Dark Yellows)*	3 fat eighths
Fabric F *(Green stripe)*	1 fat quarter

Cutting Instructions for Celebrate the Seasons

Fabric A

1 strip	4¹/2" wide	Cut into (5) 4¹/2" squares
3 strips	2¹/2" wide	

Binding

3 strips	2¹/4" wide

Cut on the wide edge of fat quarter and fat eighths
Fabric B *(4 fabrics – 1 strip from each)*

4 strips	2¹/2" wide	Cut into (12) 2¹/2" x 4¹/2" rectangles – ***matching sets of 4*** and (4) 2¹/2" squares – ***matching set of 4***

Fabric C

1 strip	2¹/2" wide	Cut into (8) 2¹/2" squares

Fabric D

1 strips	4¹/4" wide	Cut into (6) 4¹/4" squares cut in half diagonally twice
1 strip	3⁷/8" wide	Cut into (2) 3⁷/8" squares cut in half diagonally once *(corners)*

Fabric E *(3 fabrics – 1 strip from each)*

3 strips	2¹/2" wide	Cut into (12) 2¹/2" x 4¹/2" rectangles – ***matching sets of 4***

Fabric F

2 strips	2¹/2" wide	Cut into (24) 2¹/2" squares

Sewing Instructions

Draw a diagonal line on the wrong side of fabric F 2¹/2" squares
(see shortcuts).

Figure 1

*24 fabric F
2½" squares*

With right sides together, position a fabric F 2¹/2" square on the corner
of a fabric E 2¹/2" x 4¹/2" rectangle. Stitch on the pencil line. Trim seams to
¹/4" and press towards outer edge. Repeat these steps for the other corner.
Refer to Figure 2.

Figure 2

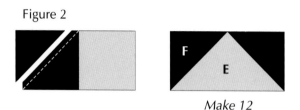

Make 12

Sew 2 fabric D triangles onto fabric B and C 2¹/2" squares as illustrated in
Figure 3. Press seams as arrows indicate, being careful not to stretch the bias
edges of the triangles.

Figure 3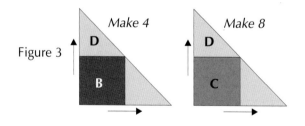

Arrange fabric A 4¹/2" squares, fabric B 2¹/2" x 4¹/2" rectangles, fabric D
corner triangles and the units you've made as illustrated in Figure 4. Sew
together to form diagonal rows. Press seams as arrows indicate.

Figure 4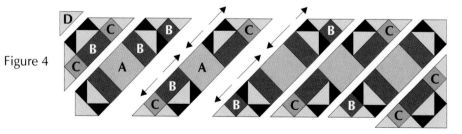

Border

Measure the length of table runner and cut 2 fabric A 2¹/2" strips to that
measurement. Sew to each side of the runner and press seams towards outer
edge. Using the same technique, apply the border to both ends.

French Bread *approximate size 51" x 18"*

Fabric Requirements: *color photo on page 17 & 54*

Fabric A *(Blue/yellow floral)*	$^2/_3$ yard	
Fabric B *(Dark blue)*	$^1/_2$	
Fabric C *(Gold floral)*	$^1/_4$	
Fabric D *(Gold texture)*	$^1/_4$	
Fabric E *(White/gold check)*	$^3/_8$	
Fabric F *(Medium blue)*	$^1/_2$ *(includes binding)*	

Cutting Instructions for French Bread

Fabric A

1	$18^1/_2$" square cut in half diagonally twice
2	$9^3/_4$" square cut in half diagonally once *(corner triangles)*

Fabric B

4 strips	$2^1/_2$" wide	Cut into (52) $2^1/_2$" squares
◣ 1 strip	$2^7/_8$" wide	Cut into (12) $2^7/_8$" squares

Fabric C

1 strip	$4^1/_2$" wide	Cut into (12) $2^1/_2$" x $4^1/_2$" rectangles

Fabric D

2 strips	$2^1/_2$" wide	Cut into (24) $2^1/_2$" squares

Fabric E

1 strip	$4^1/_2$" wide	Cut into (12) $2^1/_2$" x $4^1/_2$" rectangles
◣ 1 strip	$2^7/_8$" wide	Cut into (12) $2^7/_8$" squares

Fabric F

1 strip	$4^1/_2$" wide	Cut into (3) $4^1/_2$" squares

Binding

4 strips	$2^1/_4$" wide

◣ Do NOT cut these strips if you plan on making half square triangles by drawing a grid or using products such as Triangle Paper™

Sewing Instructions

Draw a diagonal line on the wrong side of all Fabric B 2¹/2" squares *(see shortcuts)*.

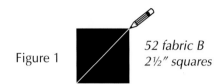

Figure 1

52 fabric B 2½" squares

With right sides together, position a fabric B 2¹/2" square on the corner of a 2¹/2" x 4¹/2" rectangle. Stitch on the pencil line, cut seam allowance to ¹/4" and press seam towards outer edge. Repeat these steps for the other corner. Refer to Figure 2.

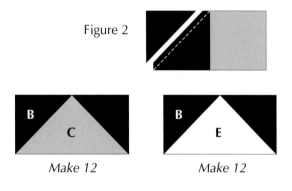

Figure 2

B C
Make 12

B E
Make 12

Sew fabric C/B units to each side of fabric F 4¹/2" square. Press seams as arrows indicate.

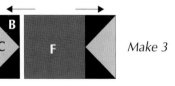

Figure 3

B C F
Make 3

Sew a fabric D 2¹/2" square onto each end of the remaining C/B units. Press seams as arrows indicate.

Figure 4 D
Make 6

Sew these sections together as illustrated in Figure 5. Press seams as arrows indicate.

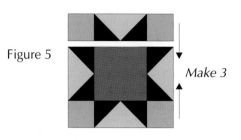

Figure 5

Make 3

Use your favorite technique to make half square triangles *(see shortcuts)* or use the following method.

Place fabric B and E 2⁷/8" squares right sides together making sure all edges are even. Cut them in half diagonally. Sew triangles together on the wide edge. Press seam towards darker fabric and trim off dog ears. Handle bias edges carefully while sewing and pressing.

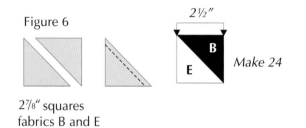

Figure 6

2½"
B
E
Make 24

2⁷/8" squares
fabrics B and E

Sew half square triangles, fabric D 2¹/2" squares and fabric B/E units together as illustrated in Figure 7. Press seams as arrows indicate.

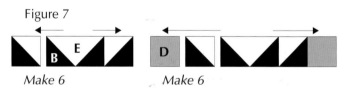

Figure 7

E B
Make 6

D
Make 6

Sew units together as illustrated in Figure 8. Press seams as arrows indicate.

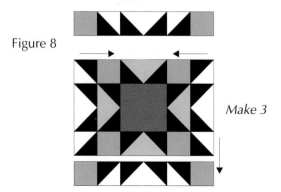

Figure 8

Make 3

With right sides together, position a fabric B 2$\frac{1}{2}$" square on the tip of a fabric A triangle as illustrated in Figure 9. Stitch on the pencil line. Cut seam allowance to $\frac{1}{4}$" and press seam towards triangle tip.

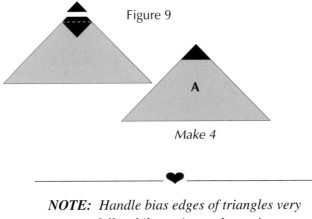

Figure 9

A

Make 4

NOTE: *Handle bias edges of triangles very carefully while sewing and pressing.*

Arrange blocks and triangles as illustrated in Figure 10 and sew together to form diagonal rows. Sew rows together, pressing while you work.

Figure 10

Tutti Frutti *approximate size 38" x 16"*

Fabric Requirements: *color photo on page 30 & 55*

Fabric A *(3 prints)*	3 fat eighths
Fabric B *(White)*	1 fat eighth
Fabric C *(Blue/white stripe)*	¼ yard
Fabric D *(Pink print)*	1 fat quarter
Fabric E *(Yellow stripe)*	¼ yard
Fabric F *(Border print)*	¼ yard
Fabric G *(Green/white dots)*	1 fat eighth
Fabric H *(Binding)*	¼ yard

Cutting Instructions for Tutti Frutti

Fabric A *(3 different fabrics)*
From EACH fabric, cut the following:

2	3¼" squares
1	2½" square

Fabric B

6	3¼" squares

Fabric C

1 strip	4⅞" wide	Cut into (6) 4⅞" squares cut in half diagonally once

---

Fabric D *(cut on the wide edge of fat quarter)*

6 strips	1¾" wide

Fabric E

3 strips	1¼" wide

Fabric F

3 strips	2½" wide

---

continued

(Cutting Instructions for Tutti Frutti continued)

Fabric G

4   2¹/₂" squares

Fabric H *(Binding)*

3 strips   2¹/₄" wide

Sewing Instructions

Measure 1¹/₄" from the diagonal center of fabric A and B 3¹/₄" squares *(indicated by the dotted line in Figure 1)* and trim corner as illustrated.

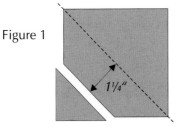

Figure 1

Trim corner from 6 fabric A and B 3¹/₄" squares

1¹/₄"

Using a sharp pencil, mark each corner of the fabric A 2¹/₂" squares from the edge as illustrated in Figure 2.

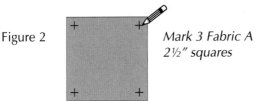

Figure 2

Mark 3 Fabric A 2½" squares

With right sides together, place fabric A 2¹/₂" square on top of a matching and trimmed 3¹/₄" square as illustrated in Figure 3. Sew in-between the marks. Backstitch a few stitches at the beginning and end of the seam.

Start and end stitching exactly at the hatch marks

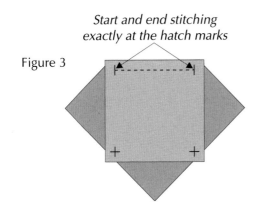

Figure 3

Repeating these steps, apply the other half of the bow tie to the opposite side of the fabric A 2¹/₂" square.

Following the same steps, apply the trimmed fabric B pieces to the remaining free sides of the fabric A square. Remember to backstitch these seams as well.

Fold bow tie unit in half so sides are even. Stitch seam starting at the outer edge, sewing towards the seam intersection and ending with a few backstitches.

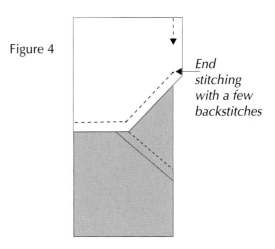

Figure 4

End stitching with a few backstitches

Repeat these steps on the remaining 3 seams.

Figure 5

Make 3

Carefully press bow ties.

Fingerpress fabric C triangles in half to mark the center. Matching crease and bow tie center seam, sew triangles onto each side of the bow tie block. Refer to Figure 6. Pay attention that the stripes are pointing in the right direction.

Press seams towards the outer edge as you work. Complete each side before going onto the next.

Figure 6

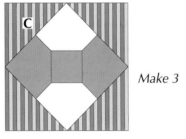

Make 3

If necessary trim blocks so edges are even.

Measure bow tie blocks and cut 6 fabric D 1³/4" strips to that measurement.

Sew strips onto sides of the bow tie blocks and press seams towards outer edge. Repeat these steps to apply fabric D strips to the top and bottom of each block. Refer to Figure 7.

Figure 7

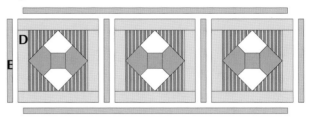

Sashing & Border

Measure blocks again and cut 4 fabric E strips (1¹/4") to that measurement. Sew these strips in-between blocks and onto each end. Press seams towards fabric E.

Measure width of the wall hanging and cut 2 strips to that measurement. Apply to the top and bottom of the wall hanging.

Outside Border

Cut 2 strips of fabric F (2¹/2") to the length and 2 strips to the width of the wall hanging measurement. *(Be sure to measure quilt through the middle.)* Sew fabric G 2¹/2" squares onto each end of the shorter outer border strips and press seams as arrows indicate in Figure 8.

Figure 8

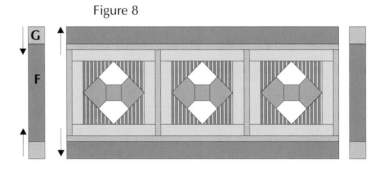

Apply top and bottom border first, pressing seams towards outer edge, then apply sides and press.

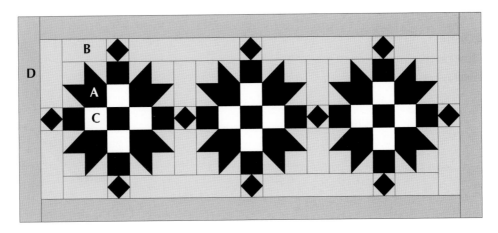

Snow Princess *approximate size 42" x 18"*

Fabric Requirements: *color photo on page 55*

Fabric A *(Navy print)*	$^{1}/_{2}$ yard
Fabric B *(Light turquoise)*	$^{3}/_{4}$
Fabric C *(White)*	$^{1}/_{8}$
Fabric D *(Medium turquoise)*	$^{5}/_{8}$ *(includes binding)*

Cutting Instructions for Snow Princess

Fabric A

1 strip	$4^{1}/_{2}$" wide	Cut into (12) $2^{1}/_{2}$" x $4^{1}/_{2}$" rectangles
2 strip	$2^{1}/_{2}$" wide	Cut into (13) $2^{1}/_{2}$" squares leave 1 strip whole
◼ 1 strip	$2^{7}/_{8}$" wide	Cut into (6) $2^{7}/_{8}$" squares

Fabric B

◼ 1 strip	$2^{7}/_{8}$" wide	Cut into (6) $2^{7}/_{8}$" squares
5 strips	$2^{1}/_{2}$" wide	Cut into (24) $2^{1}/_{2}$" squares *and* (4) $6^{1}/_{2}$" x $2^{1}/_{2}$" rectangles *and* (8) $4^{1}/_{2}$" x $2^{1}/_{2}$" rectangles *and* (4) $10^{1}/_{2}$" x $2^{1}/_{2}$" rectangles
2 strips	$1^{1}/_{2}$" wide	Cut into (40) $1^{1}/_{2}$" squares

Fabric C

1 strip	$2^{1}/_{2}$" wide

Fabric D

3 strips	$2^{1}/_{2}$" wide

Binding

3 strips	$2^{1}/_{4}$" wide

◼ Do NOT cut these strips if you plan on making half square triangles by drawing a grid or using products such as Triangle Paper™

Sewing Instructions

Draw a diagonal line on the wrong side of fabric B 2¹/2" and 1¹/2" squares *(see shortcuts)*.

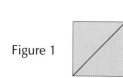

Figure 1

12 fabric B
2½" squares
40 fabric B
1½" squares

With right sides together, position a fabric B 2¹/2" square on the corner of a fabric A 2¹/2" x 4¹/2" rectangle. Stitch on the pencil line. Cut seam allowance to ¹/4" and press towards outer edge. Refer to Figure 2.

Figure 2

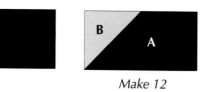

B
A

Make 12

Use your favorite technique to make half square triangles *(see shortcuts)* or use the following method.

Place fabric A and B 2⁷/8" squares right sides together making sure all edges are even. Cut them in half diagonally. Sew triangles together on the wide edge. Press seam towards darker fabric and trim off dog ears. Handle bias edges carefully while sewing and pressing.

Figure 3

2½"

A
B

Make 12

2⁷/8" squares
fabrics A and B

Sew a fabric B 2¹/2" square onto each half square triangle as illustrated in Figure 4. Press seam as arrow indicates.

Figure 4

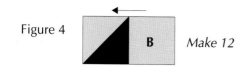

B

Make 12

Sew units together as illustrated in Figure 5 and press seam as arrow indicates.

Figure 5

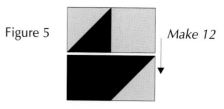

Make 12

Sew fabric A and C 2¹/2" strips together lengthwise. Press seam towards darker fabric. Cutting across the pieced strip, cut into 2¹/2" sections.

2½"

Figure 6

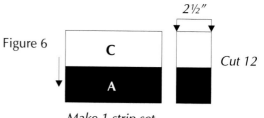

C

A

Cut 12

Make 1 strip set

Arrange sections and fabric A 2¹/2" square as illustrated in Figure 7. Sew sections into 3 horizontal rows. Press seams as arrows indicate. Sew rows together to form block.

Figure 7

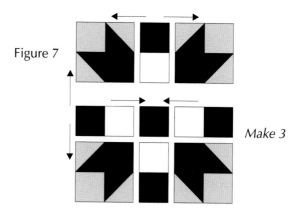

Make 3

Sashing

Starting at one corner, with right sides together, place a 1¹/₂"
fabric B square on top of a fabric A 2¹/₂" square. Stitch on the
pencil line. Press seams towards outer edge and then trim to ¹/₄".
Finish each corner before going onto the next. Refer to Figure 8.

Figure 8 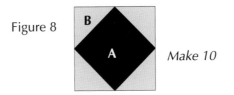 *Make 10*

Refer to Figure 9 and sew fabric B rectangles onto these units as
illustrated. Press seams as arrows indicate.

Figure 9

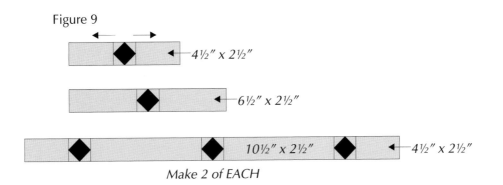

Make 2 of EACH

Sew sashing in-between blocks and then onto the outer edges.
Refer to Figure 10.

Figure 10

Outer Border

Measure the length of your table runner *(through the middle)* and
cut 2 fabric D 2¹/₂" strips to that measurement. Sew to each side
of the table runner and press seams towards outer edge. Using
the same technique, apply the outer border to each end of the
table runner.

RESOURCES

Quilting would not be what it is today without the concerted efforts of many quilt retailers. Honor their efforts by first checking with them on the availability of products before ordering directly from the manufacturer.

Other designs by Nicole Chambers

Patterns:
- Apple Pie
- Dancing in the Moonlight
- Smarter than the Average Bear
- Miss Eva's Garden
- Wild Roses from Milan
- Spring
- Summer
- Autumn
- Winter
- Classroom Sampler

Block of the Month Series:
- Family Treasures
- As Time Goes By

OOQ™ Mystery Series:
- Operation: Weather or Not
- The Rose Blooms at Midnight
- My Fine Feathered Friend

These patterns are available at your local quilt shop or from Nicole's Art to Live With, PO Box 740, Depoe Bay, OR 97341 (541) 764-2778 www.quiltmaniac.com

Products that have been mentioned in the book are as follows:

The Angler2™
Pam Bono Designs
PO Box 8247
Durango, CO 81301
800-970-5426
www.pambonodesigns.com

Triangle Paper™
Quiltime
9640 Tropical Parkway
Las Vegas, NV 89149
702-658-7988
800-982-8525
www.quiltime.com

3½" x 4"

Color scheme:

Quilt ideas:

3½" x 4"

Color scheme:

Quilt ideas:

BIBLIOGRAPHY

Albers, Joseph, *The Interaction of Color.*
New Haven: Yale University Press, 1975

Barnes, Christine, *Color: The Quilter's Guide.*
Bothell: That Patchwork Place, 1997

Color. Los Angeles: Knapp Press, 1980

Leland, Nita, *Exploring Color – Revised Edition.*
Cincinnati: North Light Books, 1998

Powell, William F., *Color And How To Use It.*
Laguna Hills: Walter Foster Publishing, 1984

INDEX

ABOUT THE AUTHOR

It became self evident very early in life that Nicole Chambers was born to be a quilter. She started building her stash at the tender age of 6 by charming all of the neighbor ladies into giving up their fabric scraps — much to the chagrin of her mother. Before starting her pattern company, Nicole's Art to Live With in 1994; Nicole used her creative design and writing skills by working for many years as a Communications Specialist for a variety of companies. Although she thoroughly enjoyed this career, when she found herself sneaking quilting books into 'the office' in plain brown wrappers, it was time to reconsider her career path. It was then that she decided to turn her talents towards the quilting world.

Nicole considers quilting to be a very important avenue of self expression and finds it no accident that so many women and men are such enthusiastic participants. It allows the creative spirit to soar while allowing us to leave a trail of memories behind to remind our loved ones just how dear they are.

She is committed to teaching and encouraging all quilters to honor their unique creativity, always coaxing them to stretch themselves a little with every quilting project. Motivated by the recognition that it can be hard to find time to indulge our passion to quilt as much as we would like to, Nicole drafts her patterns with a keen eye towards quality. She remembers well the precious moments we finally have for ourself at the end of a taxing day, or the frustration we feel when we can't figure out what the next step is and at 2:00 AM find ourself wondering if it would be reasonable to ask the telephone operator if she quilts.

Nicole and her son Aaron live on the Oregon Coast. Both enjoy the relaxed beach atmosphere as a welcome change from the metropolitan life-style they enjoyed while living on the east coast. She has won awards for both quilting and photography.